Our Father ABE

Our Father Abe

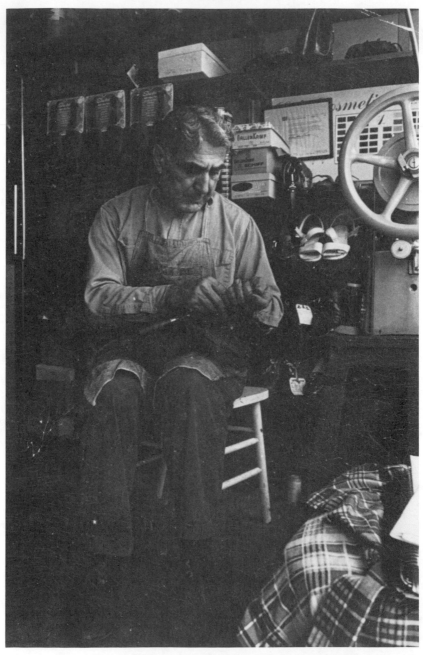

1913 - 1987

Our Father ABE

The Story of a
Deaf Shoe Repairman

Harvey L. Barash, M.D. and Eva Barash Dicker, M.S.

ABAR PRESS
Madison, Wisconsin

ISBN 0-9629634-1-0

GRAPHIC AND EDITORIAL PRODUCTION:
MONTGOMERY MEDIA, INC.
MILWAUKEE, WI.

PRINTED IN THE UNITED STATES OF AMERICA.

" . . . the prelingually deaf, unable to hear their parents, risk being severely retarded, if not permanently defective, in their grasp of language unless early and effective measures are taken. And to be defective in language, for a human being, is one of the most desperate of calamities, for it is only through language that we enter fully into our human estate and culture, communicate freely with our fellows, acquire and share information. If we cannot do this, we will be bizarrely disabled and cut off — whatever our desires, or endeavors, or native capacities."

From *Seeing Voices,* by Oliver Sacks, 1989

". . . but [Abe's] language is dreadfully poor. He cannot express himself in good English and this is because he has no foundation. He is a bright boy but many of the important subjects have been neglected, and his foundation is so poor that he has practically no ability to read even the simplest books."

Excerpted from a letter written about Abe (age 14) to Abe's mother by Mr. Bray, Superintendent of the Wisconsin School for the Deaf in Delavan, Wisconsin (December 28, 1927).

"What he could not express through the spoken word, he communicated with his shining eyes, generous heart, and strong hands."

Abe's epitaph

Dedicated

to our mother, Hilda

and

to our children

Marcy and Todd

David, Jonathan, Joshua, and Daniel

Contents

PROLOGUE

Jewish tradition teaches that the day of one's death is more important than the day of one's birth. When a child is born, his course is uncharted. There is no way to know what the future will bring. Will he perform good or bad deeds? What will be the final measure of his life? On the other hand, when a man dies, what he has done with his life is known. A full record has been created and a judgment about that life can be made.

On June 8, 1987, the day of Abe Barash's death, the world lost a remarkable man. His life was unusual, in that he overcame extreme hardship and a significant handicap to emerge successful, endowed with immense inner strength.

Abe Barash had an enormous following in his community. Those who knew him were enriched by his presence and in awe of his accomplishments. He left a remarkable legacy reflected in his work, his family, and his spirit.

Abe Barash radiated unusual warmth and grace. His strong chiseled face and his bearing were impressive. His shining eyes, never elusive, bespoke everything about him and within him. Through them his inner spirit was reflected. His face shone, the memory of his life shines, and he will be forever a shining example to those who knew him.

Yet, although he became a shining presence, he also knew intense periods of darkness. Deaf from the age of ten months and unable to articulate his thoughts and his feelings, he had experienced enormous frustration. His sister Lillian remembers the resentment he felt when he discovered at age ten that their cat could hear while he could not.

At times he felt great rage, threatening violence, though never actually inflicting it upon himself or upon others. Because he didn't know what people might be saying about him, his intelligence, or his handicap, he sometimes grew suspicious and at times even paranoid. It was not unusual for him to complain that people were talking about him or that they looked down on him. He might lash out at others inappropriately, including members of his own family, because of simple misunderstandings.

In his early married years, during the height of the Depression, he felt the crush of enormous responsibilities as he opened his own shoe repair shop, supported a wife and children, bought a house, and cared for his wife's invalid parents. His children, when they came, were wanted, yet not wanted. He was proud to be a father, but burdened by the material needs he knew his children would require.

He was deeply disturbed by his deafness and his inability to understand the English language well. He felt that he was capable of doing more with his life. He felt relegated to repairing shoes, but dreamed about how he might have been a doctor, lawyer, businessman, or even President, had he not been cursed with a profound loss of hearing. He often asked why God had punished him in this way. What had he done to deserve this life of silence, without sound or the power of the spoken word?

His moods were no different than anyone's, but they were magnified and intensified. He tended, at first, to see things in absolutes, either black or white. It was hard for him to appreciate subtle nuances or small shades of difference. His bleak periods were darker, his happy moments brighter.

While each of us possesses an enormous capacity to grow and to change, probably most of us fail to do so dramatically during our lifetimes. At an early age, we establish a certain outlook on life, and our later years become self-fulfilling prophecies of our childhood years.

At some point in the middle years of his life, Abe Barash gradually stopped fighting his handicap and began to accept his deafness. Slowly he began to change. He became less suspicious, more trusting. The bitterness disappeared and was replaced by a more mellow quality, a kindness and generosity. He became loving and content. Instead of questioning why God had caused this affliction, he found peace in his religion. An inner spiritual quality began to radiate from his strong face.

The exact reasons for these changes are not clear. It may be that as his children grew older and provided a link for him to the hearing world, Abe was able to see how great an influence he had on others. He was grateful to see his children, and later his grandchildren, study at universities, and this gave him tremendous satisfaction. He felt partially responsible for their successes and especially proud when they chose professions related to his handicap. He had inspired both family and casual acquaintances to become interested in Sign Language and the problems of the deaf. He had inspired others to seek service in the field of medicine, and still others to devote their lives to Judaism. Further, he sensed that he had the profound respect of his children, grandchildren, and the entire community.

In his later years, instead of allowing his darker moods to prevail, he accepted the silent world within which he lived. He had steadily achieved a quiet dignity and he had developed into a man larger than life, a man about whom legends might be written.

He is gone now. We can no longer see his handsome, expressive face or touch his beautiful and powerful hands, but we can honor his memory. We believe that our father's story is worth sharing, particularly with those who are disabled by deafness or other impairments, for his life demonstrates that a seemingly insignificant and humble man can indeed touch many other lives and make a difference in this world.

For this reason we decided to prepare a record of his life in words and pictures. In this book we hope to tell the life story of our beloved father so that his example will endure for us, for our children, and for future generations. His story is unusual, not only as a story of success against great odds, but also as an example of man's great capacity for change.

H.L.B. and E.B.D.

In a sense, I feel like an interloper because I really did not live with my brother Abe for any long periods of time. I lived instead in his "sphere of influence." Abe left for Delavan when I was not yet a year old and returned home only for vacations. These vacations were times for excited preparations, of great joy and boundless excitement. How I hung on him, followed him about–what a pest I was! He was so strong, could swing me about and lift me to the ceiling. I loved having a big brother, but soon he was gone again.

Nonetheless, his presence was felt throughout the house every hour of every day as I was growing up. To my mother he was truly a light unto her life, the only son. I remember the many packages and letters which went forth from our house to Delavan, the long stories my mother told about Abe, and her deep sighs as she longed for his presence and anguished over his deafness and the hearing loss of my sister. She spent many hours in reverie over "what if my children had not been afflicted?"

I recall sitting at the kitchen table "writing letters" to Abe long before I knew how to spell, filling pages with newly learned alphabet letters, begging my parents or sister to tell me what words my letters had formed. He was always in our minds then as his influence has pervaded many lives since.

The lost potential, the "might have been" so poignantly penetrated my life that it became a driving force propelling me to achieve. I felt obligated to make up to my parents for the son and daughter whose handicaps could not allow them to fulfill their potential. In a sense it was a form of "survivor guilt" which made it essential that I justify my good fortune in being "normal." Why was I not among the children with hearing loss? Did I really deserve to hear?

As a child with a mission I felt very special, the only child born in the United States, and "normal" at that. At the same time this made me different, bringing a sense of not belonging to the other family members who had immigrated so far, experienced so much, and were not of this land. This feeling of isolation has never left me.

Brother Abe was really a legend in my life. He was, indeed, bigger than life, idealized and adored. His handsome face, strong body, and winsome smile reached many hearts, capturing the love and the imagination of a broad spectrum of people who were similarly inspired to reach for stars beyond their perceived selves so that they, too, could "make up to Abe for his lost hearing." I often wonder what he would have accomplished had he been a doctor, lawyer, executive? I suspect less than he did in his shop on Regent Street, repairing soles and re-establishing respectability to worn-out shoes. He met and touched people from all walks of life, making an impression that lasted longer than that of the average professional. His industry, reliability, and the work of what our mother used to call his *goldene hendt* (golden hands) were extraordinarily impressive.

The world now has his children, grandchildren, in-laws, nieces, and nephews, all of whom in one way or another are trying to make up for Abe's handicap. They have become doctors, teachers of the deaf, interpreters, leaders in promoting understanding of the deaf, and responsible, contributing members of society.

Sometimes I imagine writing a letter to my big brother where I would say:

"It is a better world, dear Abe, because of your bountiful life. We miss you but your work goes on in your progeny and in your 'sphere of influence.' Thank you for never giving up the struggle. We love you and the inspiration which you have provided."

Your baby sister,
Lucille

NOTES FROM JOHN PATRICK HUNTER

Dear Harvey and Eva:

I knew your father only casually before I read *Our Father Abe: The Story of a Deaf Shoe Repairman.* Even the occasional meetings that involved bringing either my shoes or my wife's to the shop and later in his life admiring his jogging in the University Shell gave me a hint of a strong personality.

But the son and daughter recollections of life with Abe Barash and the excellent biographical background of his childhood in Russia and his later life in Wisconsin is marked with a good sense of his individuality and an acute sensitivity to your father's struggle to overcome his handicaps.

Abe's mother comes through as the quintessential Jewish Mother. It was tragic that a mother's concern and a son's rebellion and need for independence caused a split between Abe and his parents when he reached adulthood.

Especially strong are the details of Abe's life before his marriage that were constructed through interviews with family and acquaintances. The writing makes a reporter envious because it portrays a skillful mixture of personal triumph and adversity. The same kind of moving saga is spelled out in the lives of untold millions of immigrants who passed through Ellis Island to a new life in a strange and often hostile land.

I thought I knew much about Wisconsin, but the report of Abe's schooling at Delavan opened a new vista to me, as did the manner in which the deaf were educated.

Abe's courtship and marriage, and here again Freda's role in pulling the strings, are very well done. It is no wonder Abe felt "out of control" as Freda continued to make decisions about his life.

The manuscript gives an excellent account of the Jewish network in Madison which I only dimly perceived, even though I knew of the leading role Jews have played in Madison's history and in its cultural and business life.

The cutline under the wedding day photograph has a ring of poetry: "They marched down the aisle to a musical interlude they could not hear and watched Rabbi Cashdan as he silently moved his lips, not understanding the vows being spoken or the hopeful and inspiring words."

Nothing could more eloquently spell out Barash's triumph as well as the handicap of living in a world that they could sense acutely but whose rhythms and music they could only imagine.

The manuscript excels in delineating a part of the whole. The Barash family, making friends, Abe's work in the Regent Street Shop that was a landmark to all who both knew him and admired his determination to succeed.

The photography adds a heartwarming dimension to the biography, including the wonderful picture of the new arrivals aboard ship in 1921, and Abe and Hilda's wedding picture. It is moving. There is also a sense of pride and reluctance to give up their daughter in Abe and Hilda's faces as they escort Eva down the aisle in Eva's wedding picture.

The manuscript ends with the same moving sensitivity with which it began. There's a warm feeling of love that tempers the sadness of death. Abe must have drawn strength from his family and that strength certainly must have softened his final hours of sadness and depression.

Harvey and Eva, this manuscript cries out for publication. I knew the Barashes only tangentially before I began reading it. Now I feel like a member of the family. If it can do that for this hardbitten newspaper man, it certainly must have an appeal to all who treasure the triumph of life over adversity and the dividends that love can bring.

John Patrick Hunter

ACKNOWLEDGMENTS

Portions of this book were reconstructed from a series of interviews. We are particularly indebted to our mother, Abe's older sister Lillian, younger sister Lucille, and sister-in-law Rebecca. We also owe thanks to his many deaf friends, through whom we have come to know our father in his younger years. Other parts of the book were based on personal memories, as well as research, where applicable, to corroborate our impressions.

We are thankful for the early helpful and sensitive editing provided by Harvey's wife, Trudy.

We also owe special thanks to Mary Huntington, Susan Montgomery, and Cynthia Vance of Montgomery Media, Inc., for their help with editing, graphic design, and layout.

We appreciate the critical comments made by the readers of our original manuscript: Sandy Brusin, Laura Greene, John Patrick Hunter, Marc Kornblatt, Larry Newman, Simcha Prombaum, and Gretchen Schoff.

We are indebted to Robert Buchanan for bringing to our attention correspondence between Superintendent Bray and Abe's family, housed at the Wisconsin State Historical Society. His timely discovery of this correspondence greatly enhanced the content of this book. These letters were preserved along with several other selected sets of letters as examples of correspondence between the school authorities and the students or their families.

Finally, we wish to thank the many people who participated in interviews or provided other recollections and input: Bill Angel, Harvey and Dorothy Boldt, Peter Chortek, Rabbi Charles Feinberg, Wendy Gordon, Mrs. Hoffman, Lola Horgen, John Kuglitsch, Phil Lev, Sarah Manis Locke, Clarence Miller, Peter Miller, Sam Onheiber, Francis Perry, Harry Row, Eva Schrank, Harold Sweet, Leonard Sweet, Nancy Miles Townsend, Merle Neefe Treit, and Alice Walser. We apologize for any omissions from this list.

Part I

EARLY YEARS

CHAPTER 1

RUSSIAN CHILDHOOD

In 1913 in the village of Delinkas along the southwestern border of Russia, a son was born to Peter and Freda Barash. This tiny village or *shtetl*, as it was called in Yiddish, was located near the city of Kiev. Abraham Morris was their second child and their first-born son. His name was a proud reminder of Judaism's first patriarch, and it was expected that he would carry out the Jewish traditions bequeathed to him by generations that had come before him.

Abe, or little Avrum, as he came to be called, was a robust infant remarkable for his dark, shining eyes. He was blessed with good health until ten months of age when he suddenly developed a high fever. No medical help could be found to control the fever and relieve his discomfort. When at last the fever subsided, Abe was no longer able to hear any sound. He was left with permanent nerve damage resulting in a profound hearing loss. For the rest of his life he would have to rely solely on his eyes to understand and learn about the world.

His sister Lillian, almost three, had also been ill some months earlier with a chronic ear infection. Following that illness her family noticed that she could not hear well, although she was still able to understand the sounds of human speech.

The children's lives had been altered forever. Abe, his family's symbol of hope for a better future and the continuation of the Judaic tradition, no longer would be able to fulfill the religious obligations of a Jewish son. Learning to read Hebrew now seemed an impossible task.

Freda was devastated, more so because she was at that time alone in Delinkas with her children. When Abe was only a few months old, Peter, his father, had traveled to America in order to earn money there for his family's passage from Russia. Lillian remembers what her mother had told her about her father's absence:

> My father had always wanted to go to America and my mother agreed. No one knew much about America. My father had worked in a factory in Russia. He did not like his job and he wanted to go. So Mother encouraged him to go first and earn some money. He went alone just before the war broke out. He was also afraid that he might have to go into the army. The war was going on . . . no mail from him. We did not hear from him for seven years.

Life in Delinkas

Life in Delinkas was difficult for everyone who lived in revolution-torn Russia at the beginning of the twentieth century. Jews and gentiles alike were poor and worked hard to eke out an existence that would be far below the poverty level by today's standards. People lived side by side in relative harmony, helping and protecting one another when it was possible. Whenever the Czar's soldiers raided Delinkas, the townspeople scattered to the nearby forest where they would hide until the soldiers left. Freda's family hid in the forest many times, and Lillian remembers feeling frightened but safe, because the relatives were all there with them. Freda's sisters and brothers, Haika, Nehama, Motl, Pesah, and Sonia,

Abe and his sister Lillian as young children living in Delinkas, not far from Kiev. Their lives had been forever altered because of their hearing loss.

all lived close by. Peter's mother, Chaia, and his only sister, Sorah, were also nearby. Lillian remembers:

> We all protected each other. The people were very poor. The soldiers killed old people. I don't know if they were Jews or not. Mother grabbed us and took us away. Everyone protected us.
>
> In the house all the beds, the sofa, and the stove were in one room. We slept near the stove in the winter. Abe slept with me in the same bed. We cooked and ate and slept in one room. There was no glass on the windows. There were bars on the windows. The toilet was outside. We brought the wooden tub in for baths. When we were done we took the tub out and threw the water away. Everyone used the same water. There was no privacy. We only had curtains, and if someone came to visit, we pulled the curtains.

Although the people of Delinkas had no money they bartered for their everyday needs. They traded flour for seeds and grew all of their own food. They made their own butter and then used the buttermilk and sour cream, the by-products of the butter-churning process. The diet staples were the same for everyone. The family grew potatoes and preserved them in the ground during the winter. They made bread with flour they had ground themselves.

Sabbath in the *shtetl* was awaited eagerly by every Jewish family. On Fridays, the smells of challah (specially prepared bread for the Sabbath) and cinnamon rolls pervaded the small houses. The children were bathed in a round wooden tub on Friday afternoon in preparation for welcoming the Sabbath Queen. Abe and Lillian had the all-important task of carrying pails of water to fill it.

The Sabbath meal was a festive one in even the poorest of families. In Abe's home the meal began as Freda's brothers and sisters and their children gathered around the table to light candles welcoming the Sabbath, a day of rest from the weekly toil. Blessings were chanted over the wine and bread, thanking God for his goodness, specially prepared foods were eaten, and *Zmirot* (songs) were sung as a joyous end to the meal. On the following day the entire family walked to the shul (synagogue) to chant the Sabbath prayers. Abe's early Sabbath memories were the beginnings of the strong Jewish feelings he would carry within him for the rest of his life.

Freda

Freda Pevnick, Abe's mother, was the oldest child in her family. When she was only eleven, she left her home for the big city of Odessa to work in a factory as a seamstress. She worked there for three years until she was fourteen. It was her responsibility to earn money so that her younger brothers and sisters could go to school and study. Freda too had dreamed of an education, but since she was the oldest and had to work, she would never have that opportunity herself.

In 1910, when she was twenty, Freda married Peter and began to work in a store owned by her mother-in-law, Chaia Barash. She learned quickly and before long understood how to make a small profit. In her early twenties it was common for Freda to make her way to Odessa to buy goods for the store in spite of the fighting that continued near her village and in the countryside. It was not unusual for her to be gone for several days at a time and her family constantly feared for her safety. Freda went in place of the men, who were needed to protect the village from the soldiers. Her reputation for courage among the villagers of Delinkas was well deserved, and later her fierce determination to go to America to improve her life was not surprising to those who knew her well.

The *Groys Knaker*

As Abraham grew, the aunts and uncles vied for the

privilege of caring for him when Freda had to be gone overnight. They called him the *groys knaker,* meaning great head,
or brain, because he was so clever. Lillian recalls:

> Everybody loved him. They were just crazy about
> him. If he would suddenly appear, my aunt would say,
> "Oy . . . here comes the *groys knaker.*" They called him
> that because he was so smart and so cute. The way he
> was talking he made everybody laugh. He would come
> and say like this (gesture of a key turning). That
> meant the door was locked, and then he would say,
> "Wooooo" (gesture of hands held out in despair, eye-
> brows raised, shaking head from side to side). That
> meant nobody was home, so they would have to take
> care of him. He would say, "No mama . . . went to buy,"
> using homemade signs.

Abe loved spending time with the relatives because
he knew they would give him delicious foods to eat and the
attention that he loved. He was very aware of the hypnotic
power he had over his family members. They would have
done anything for this charismatic boy who could not speak,
this boy with sparkling eyes.

Although Abe was not able to hear, he continued to
absorb the daily activity around him with keen perception.
He loved watching his grandfather and other members of his
family build things and in no time at all he was able to mimic
exactly what he had been watching. The *groys knaker* often
lived up to his name. He used to strut around as if he were in
charge of the town and all the people. If his mind was idle too
long, he would become mischievous. It was obvious to the
villagers that he was precocious and that "Boozie," as his
mother Freda was affectionately known, need not worry about
her son's future success. Abe also believed this about himself
and took delight in tapping his head with his forefinger.
People asked Boozie what Abe meant by this gesture, and she
explained that Abe was trying to tell them that he was smart.

His earliest visual memories included births, deaths, holidays, birthday celebrations, weddings, and funerals. Freda continued to invent gestures to communicate events of the life cycle and daily ritual to Abe. The "home sign" gestures might include bowing a violin in order to tell Abe there was going to be a wedding, or a miming gesture slicing the neck to let him know that the rabbi was coming to slaughter the chickens in the manner prescribed by Jewish law. In this primitive way, Abe began to understand the world about him.

Education

Freda clearly understood the importance of education. She learned of a nearby Russian school to which she brought Lillian and Abe, but the methods were crude and the teacher harsh. Lillian recalls:

> The school was so far away. Abe was five and I was seven. We went to school, but Abe couldn't learn. The teacher was so mean. She sent me to the corner and grabbed children. We were so scared. She was very, very strict. Mother didn't think I should go to that school. Abe didn't go either, because the teacher couldn't teach him.

Freda took them out of school after a short time and then arranged for Nahama and Haika to teach the children Yiddish. After many attempts Abraham learned to speak the words *tante* (aunt), *bruder* (brother), and *shvester* (sister), along with some words used for labeling foods. So it was that Abe began "communicating" with a combination of gestures, words, and short Yiddish phrases.

Uncle Motl, who was well educated in Hebrew, challenged himself to teach Abraham to pronounce *Alef, Bet, and Gimel,* the first three letters of the Hebrew alphabet. Abe studied Motl's lip movements in the pronunciation of *Alef* and *Bet* and easily mimicked the movements. He had a harder time with *Gimel,* because the beginning sound, hard "g," like "k," is made in the back of the throat and cannot be seen easily to be imitated. Abraham struggled and Motl struggled. As a final effort Motl placed Abe's hand on his throat, hoping Abe would feel the vibrations produced in the back of the throat that could not be seen or heard.

Abe, sensing that he could not learn what others appeared to learn so easily, darted out the door and began to run. Lillian recalls:

> Abe got mad because he couldn't learn the *Gimel,* so he ran away. He ran outside; it was winter and the snow was high. Motl ran after him because he didn't want him to get sick. Motl caught him and kissed him. Abe understood and hugged himself—that meant that Motl still loved him.

Freda Barash, also known as "Boozie," circa 1920. She hoped that somehow in America it might be possible for Abe and Lillian to receive a better education and she believed that she might find doctors who would be able to help her children hear again.

This early frustration foretold of feelings buried deeply within which he would carry with him for a lifetime. As a young adult he would continue to run away from situations that frustrated him.

Until he began to learn Sign Language at the age of fourteen, Abe was never able to indicate more than his immediate needs. His mother and sister Lillian understood his gestures and short Yiddish phrases very well, but more abstract communication about his thoughts and feelings was seldom possible. It was particularly difficult for Freda to explain the difference between right and wrong, because Abe's understanding was limited to what he could see. The cause and effect of certain actions became clear to him only by his own experimentation, never by someone else's explanation. All Freda could do was teach "basic" right from wrong. She could never hope to convey the gray areas between the two extremes. It was not uncommon to see Abe race around the kitchen table, running from his mother, when he believed he was going to be punished or spanked. Often she could not explain why she was upset with him or why she felt he might be in danger. The look on her face was one of fear for him rather than anger. She behaved as she did to protect him, whether or not he understood.

Departure from Russia

Freda longed for something better and although she knew that she would miss her family in Russia, she looked forward to a different life for her children in America. She hoped that in America it might be possible for Abe and Lillian to be educated, and she believed that she might find doctors who could help her children hear again. She waited to hear from Peter as Abe turned seven and Lillian nine.

After seven years, following the end of World War I, letters from America finally began getting through to the family. Lillian recalls:

My father wrote that he had sent one thousand dollars.
My mother never got it. He said he wrote many letters.
We did not get them, nor the thousand dollars . . . so
we had to go to a certain place to get money from him
. . . I think we went to Warsaw to get the money.

When, after many months, the money still had not
arrived in Delinkas, Freda felt she could not wait any longer.
She knew it was becoming increasingly dangerous to remain
in Russia, because of the revolution and the pogroms in which
towns were ravaged and thousands of people were killed.
Concerned for the safety of her family, she decided to travel
to Warsaw and try to smuggle enough Russian money out of
the country to use until they received money from her husband.

One night at midnight in November 1920, she left for
Warsaw with her two sleepy children. When they arrived at
the Russian border several days later, the soldiers were rough
with Freda as they were with most people leaving the country. They questioned her aggressively about her money. The
money was sewn into the children's underwear, but luckily
the soldiers did not think of looking there. Freda gradually
evolved a strategy with Lillian which was to prove useful at
several checkpoints. Freda would blink her eyes hard and
suddenly Lillian, on cue, would begin to scream and thrash at
Abe, who would also begin to scream. The beleaguered soldiers would reluctantly allow the family to move on to the
next village without checking their belongings thoroughly.
Lillian recalls:

When we left Delinkas, the soldiers checked everyone. They yelled at us, "What are you doing, do you
have money hidden in there?" I was screaming and
crying. Then the soldiers looked at us and said, "Oh,
a couple of babies . . . go!"
We stopped in another place and the soldiers
asked if we had any money . . . Mother blinked her

eyes and that meant we should cry. I shoved Abe and we both started screaming and crying as a distraction.

Later Mother asked how I knew what she wanted. I looked at her eyes and I *knew*. Very clever. . . it wasn't planned, but I got the idea of what she wanted. The money was sewn under our underwear. When we left, we couldn't bring a thing. No candles, not a thing.

All along the way peasants took the travelers into their homes. Occasionally the three had to run from one village to the next for fear of being caught, but eventually they made it to the next leg of their journey. Sometime in February, after nearly three months of traveling and hiding, the family arrived in Warsaw.

Lillian and Abe could not understand why they had left Russia. All they knew for certain was that Freda was worried. She looked worried and spoke quietly. The children longed for familiar faces, and Freda tried to explain that she had encouraged the other relatives to come, but they had refused. None of her brothers and sisters wanted to leave, and forty years later, Freda and Peter would remain the only two members of their immediate family to have left Russia and come to America.

Warsaw

In Warsaw the family again was helped by people who hid them. Conditions were bad, as Lillian recalls:

It was cold. We hid in the basements. It was terrible but the people who hid us were kind to us. They were not all Jewish. They were German or Ukrainian. My mother told them we had run away from Delinkas. We went anyplace we could. I was so scared. There were rats in the basement. We had to be quiet.

The little family lived for several months in a rooming house. Freda eventually received the money from America and spent her days cautiously exchanging it for currency that could be used to buy tickets, passports, and clothing for the voyage to America. Lillian and Abe waited alone in their room for long hours until she returned.

One day Abraham suddenly vanished from the rooming house and no one knew where he had gone. Lillian recalls:

> He just disappeared . . . he was missing. So my mother called the police and told them a deaf boy was missing. We looked all over, but couldn't find him. The next day he came walking in the house. We asked him where he had been. He gestured that he went to a little boy's house, but we never knew where he had been. How did he know how to get back to the rooming house? He knew!

Abe's deafness complicated an already difficult situation. Freda worried about him, and Lillian remembers seeing her frequently pray for him:

> She prayed all the time so hard for him. She was praying and hoping. She was always telling me to watch him.

Lillian describes the train from Warsaw to Antwerp as hot and crowded. There were soldiers everywhere, and no room to sit down, so Abe and Lillian sat on their suitcases and held on tightly to their mother.

The port city of Antwerp teemed with activity with people running in every direction. Many hoped to secure passage on a ship bound for America, and Freda was among them. She worried that she might not have enough money for tickets and that she would not be able to make herself understood. She had been advised that it would be best to purchase middle-class tickets to escape the closer scrutiny given to passengers holding the cheapest tickets.

She worried most about Abraham. She knew that while America had opened its gates to immigrants, quotas still existed to keep those people out who could not support themselves or who might find themselves on the public welfare rolls. Lillian, with her less severe hearing loss, was able to carry on an intelligent conversation with little difficulty, but Abraham spoke poorly. He was bright enough, but most people would not understand his vocal sounds. Freda agonized and wondered how she would be able to persuade the authorities that his deafness need not cause him to become a public ward. As part of her plan, she used gestures to explain to Abraham that he was not to speak or gesture at all when other people were around.

Passage to America

In the spring of 1921, Freda was finally able to secure passage on a ship from Antwerp to New York. The voyage to America took eleven days. The ship's movement caused Freda to become very ill, which frightened Lillian and Abe—what would happen to them if they were left alone to fend for themselves? Everything was new to them and their mother's presence was the only comfort they had. Several passengers brought tea to Freda, and the children took turns staying by her side until she was well again.

The weather during the voyage was beautiful, and the two children had great fun playing with the other children on board. One day a whale was sighted close to the ship, and Lillian and Abe were very frightened—they had never seen a creature that big.

Freda tried to reassure them that they were safe, but neither child was convinced. Abe was particularly terrified for he could see passengers screaming and running but could not hear the calm of his mother's voice as she attempted to soothe him.

The passengers in the ship's middle class soon were charmed by Abe, the *groys knaker*. They did not suspect that he was deaf, since he could make out some words on their lips if they spoke Yiddish. In fact, many languages were spoken on the ship, and gesturing was an accepted form of communication. Abe's gestures appeared perfectly natural to this diverse population. Lillian recalls:

> They all thought he could hear, because he could read my lips and my mother's lips. They were talking back and forth and using their hands, too. Nobody knew he was deaf. They were all gesturing, because they spoke different languages.

Towards the end of the voyage, one of the passengers discovered that Abe was deaf and loudly identified him to the others as *"Shtum, shtum"* meaning, "Deaf, deaf." In no time at all, rumor spread that one of the passengers had a deaf child on board. The prevailing collective opinion of the passengers was that Abe would surely have to go back to Russia.

Frightened beyond words, Freda kept Abe in the cabin while she prayed desperately. Fearing the worst for Abraham, Freda wrote a letter to Peter, who was in Wisconsin, pleading with him to come to New York to meet them. She sent the letter with the first small boatload of passengers heading for Ellis Island. Lillian recalls:

> My mother wrote a letter on the boat, dropped the letter to the people who went first and asked someone to mail it. Someone caught the letter. Mother had no stamp and just hoped my father would get the letter.

Freda vowed that Abraham would never be sent back even if she had to jump into the Atlantic Ocean from the shores of America as a final act of desperation. Turning back was simply not part of her plan.

This photograph, a family treasure, was taken in 1921 on the ship when Freda and her two children arrived at Ellis Island. Abe is sitting in the third row on the extreme right in a straw hat and Lillian is standing next to an adult in the same row near the far left.

Ellis Island

On Ellis Island the authorities discovered that Abraham could not hear, but the extent of his handicap was not clear. A decision was made to assess his capabilities with an intelligence test. Abraham was taken off to a small room by himself, while Freda waited and hoped. Lillian recalls:

> They called us to the office. The doctor asked my age and name and I told him, but when he asked Abraham, he didn't know. He didn't understand, so that's why he had to go in the room. I knew what to answer, but Abe didn't understand.
> They asked him to come into a room alone and they didn't want anyone else to go along. In five minutes he came out. My mother was frightened because it was done so fast. The man said, "He's okay, you can go. He may enter."

Freda hugged Abe and kissed him many times. They were free to make their way in this strange new country. Later, when they were alone, Freda asked Abe what he had done in the small testing room. Abe shrugged and didn't seem to be able to tell her. Years later, when he was able to communicate in Sign Language and to write some English, Freda learned that he had worked some puzzles, mixing them up and then putting them together, all integral parts of nonverbal intelligence tests.

Peter arrived to attest that this was indeed the family for whom he had been waiting these seven years. At first Abe was afraid of the stranger with the brush mustache whom Freda called *Tate;* he had no childhood memories of his father, who had left Russia when Abe was only a few months old, and he peered at him cautiously from behind his mother's skirts. Abe's attention to Peter was soon replaced by the novelty of a streetcar ride and his first ice cream cone. He couldn't get enough ice cream and kept asking for "more,

more, more." Freda warned him that he would get a stomach ache *("Avava, avava")*. Abe lipread the word *"avava"* and immediately refused the ice cream, as he had experienced the pain of a stomach ache and remembered it well. Peter was impressed that Abe was able to derive meaning from a word he read on his mother's lips. Later, when Abe wanted to run across the street, Peter held on to him and imitating Freda, said *"Avava, avava"* to try to frighten him to stay.

The family spent five days in New York, overawed by the skyscrapers and the pace of the city. Before the family left the city, Peter bought everyone new "American" clothes. They were soon on their way to Chicago by train and then on to Fond du Lac, Wisconsin. The trip from New York to Fond du Lac was long, particularly for young Abe who did not understand where his family was going. He entertained himself on the long trip by blowing up paper bags and then popping them loudly. This was a noise he could feel, and he delighted in seeing the reactions on other people's faces at the sound of the pop. When the conductor tried to quiet Abe down, he discovered that the young boy was deaf and asked Freda questions about her son. The passengers on the train were curious as well, and instead of becoming angry, they seemed to understand Abe's attempts at attention-getting. Even this mischievous behavior could not get him into trouble.

CHAPTER 2

GROWING UP IN AMERICA

After seven years of waiting and seven more months of traveling, the family had finally been reunited. No one could have dreamed in 1913 that nearly eight years would pass before Abe's father, Peter Barash, would see his family again. Abe was already eight years old and Lillian was nearly ten when they arrived by train at the tiny Wisconsin town that was to become their home.

Fond du Lac

Fond du Lac is located in the eastern part of Wisconsin, north of Wisconsin's largest city, Milwaukee. Rich farmlands surround the small community. The town suited the Barash family well; it offered a stability unknown to them in Russia. Births, deaths, and marriages were recorded in the Fond du Lac County Courthouse located on the town's Main Street. On the same street, in the heart of town, the Retlaw Hotel welcomed paying guests, and the *Fond du Lac Commonwealth Reporter* printed the daily news. The townspeople went about their daily business unbothered by soldiers or police or by the thought of a pogrom. It was a new world. The Barashes, like other immigrant families, strove hard to assimilate into the culture of this small midwestern town while at the same time retaining their own ethnic identity and traditions.

Prior to his family's arrival Peter had lived in several Wisconsin towns, most recently in nearby Sheboygan. There he had boarded with an established Jewish family, but he decided to move to Fond du Lac when his family arrived. It was far enough away from Sheboygan for Peter to establish himself independently and close enough for him to keep up his connections in the scrap metal and junk peddling business.

The family had no place to live when they first arrived in Fond du Lac. One Jewish family with a large home invited them to stay there while they looked for a place to live. After

The reunited Barash family after Freda and her children arrived in the United States. From left to right, Lillian, Peter, Freda, and Abe. The picture was taken in Fond du Lac, Wisconsin, circa 1923.

three months they bought a house with an unoccupied store in the front. While Peter continued peddling by horse and wagon, Freda established a clothing business in this store.

Little by little, the Barashes became known in the town and people took note of Abe's quick wit and intelligence. Peter was as astonished as his friends to see how much Abe understood. According to Lillian, her father did not appear to feel badly about having a deaf son. He continually commented on Abe's brightness and kept asking Freda how it was that Abe could understand so much.

On the other hand, direct communication between Abe and his father was difficult. Peter often needed Freda or Lillian to help him understand what Abe was saying, and although Peter was known to be a very gentle man, he did at times resort to using a belt to discipline Abe. Lillian remembers:

> He used the belt if Abe didn't behave. Sometimes Abe didn't listen. My mother and father never spanked me. I always listened. Abe used to run around the table and my father used to run after him. Abe was screaming for my mother. He held on to my mother tightly because he thought my father would spank him again.

Early Schooling

Once the family was settled, Freda took the children to the neighborhood school where Lillian was put into a class with children who had normal hearing. Her hearing loss was minimal and she was able to interact with and learn from hearing children. Abe was put into a class with eight to ten deaf children of differing ages. There he was given more concentrated attention, since he would have to learn by relying on his eyes to lipread what was being said.

Lipreading the connected sounds of any language is a difficult task, and much of what is lipread is educated guesswork. But when a familiar language is being spoken it is possible to anticipate words, phrases, or sentences. Suddenly Abe's task became that of lipreading a foreign language, English, without ever seeing a familiar word on his teacher's lips. It was like having to learn Japanese through a sound-proof glass-enclosed room by watching a native Japanese speaker through the glass. Abe's *shtetl* Yiddish was useless, and he had nothing to replace it.

Nevertheless, Abe liked going to school, and he loved to play games once he had figured out the rules. He also loved to race with Lillian to school and to run faster than she did; she would always pretend that he was the winner so that he would feel happy. Once another child brought a bicycle to school. Abe really wanted the bike, so he simply rode it home. When Freda asked him where he had gotten it he indicated through mime and gestures that he had just decided to take it for himself. His mother insisted that he take it back, but Abe resisted. He wanted to keep it. After many hours Freda was able to make him understand that the bike had to go back to its owner and that he would need money if he wanted to buy a bike for himself.

Selling Newspapers

Before long Abe figured out a way to earn that money. He would sell papers like the paper boy on the corner. Lillian remembers:

> He gestured that he saw a boy selling papers, saying, "Paper, paper, paper," and then getting money for them. He wanted to do it. So Mother said, "Okay, if you want to sell papers, you can." Abe was so excited. He said, "Yes, paper, paper, paper." He sold the *Fond du Lac Reporter*.

Even at this early age his ambition to succeed was evident. Soon Abe became a familiar sight on Main Street, as he walked up and down repeating his own version of "Paper, paper, paper." People responded and were eager to help this boy who tried so hard to compete with the others; he was industrious, active, and always on the lookout for more opportunities. It was not long before Abe figured out that if he went down to the early morning train before school started, he could make even more sales. Lillian explains:

> At four o'clock in the morning, when he was only nine or ten, he got up to sell papers. Mother asked him where he was going, and he answered, "Train, train, whoooooooo." That was a whistle. Mother said, "No, no, no," and he said, "Yes, yes, yes," and he ran away to the train.

Once a customer did not have enough money for the daily newspaper and asked Abe to follow her to her office for the money. For the first time, Abe learned about the offices in downtown Fond du Lac, and soon he began to frequent all the offices he could. Lillian remembers:

> The other boys copied him, but the people in the office told them they were sorry; they had promised to buy from the deaf boy. Wherever he went, he learned. He sold the most papers and he won prizes. He won a bike and roller skates.

He had become an entrepreneur by the age of ten.

Little Progress

Abe worked hard selling newspapers and at other odd jobs around town, but he grew increasingly frustrated by his deafness and his inability to express himself. He began to understand how different he was from other children. When he observed that even their pet cat could hear, Lillian remembers how he reacted:

When Abe was about ten years old, we had a cat in our house. One day Abe said, "Mama, cat hear! Why can the cat hear, and I can't hear?" That upset my mother so much. He kept asking, "The cat can hear ... me, no. Why? Why?"

Although it was evident to everyone who knew Abe that he was very bright and clever, he made limited progress in school during the next four years due to language problems. He was not a successful lipreader, and this was the only teaching method used for deaf students in the regular public schools.

Abe's teacher called Freda in to discuss his future. Freda knew that Abe must prepare for a trade and that Fond du Lac had little to offer him. She had heard about the

Abe's ambition was evident even at an early age; by age ten he had become an entrepreneur. But he was continually frustrated by his deafness.

Wisconsin School for the Deaf, a residential school in Delavan, about 130 miles south of Fond du Lac. At Delavan the subjects were taught in Sign Language, a manual method of communication that was not at that time fully accepted by educators outside the residential school setting. Lipreading was also emphasized. The school offered vocational training in printing, woodworking, shoe repairing, and agriculture.

Freda and Peter wanted Abe to be self-supporting in his adulthood, so after many long hours of discussion, they eventually decided to send him to Delavan to learn a trade. The decision to send Abraham away was heart-wrenching, as it meant he would be leaving his family and the small Jewish community which had provided security and stability in a world still foreign to him. He would not be able to come home more than twice during the school year, since the family had no car and little money for train or bus transportation. Even worse, this major decision and its probable benefits would be impossible to explain to Abe. They were certain Abe would feel rejected and angry, but they knew that they must put aside their anguish and Abe's anger for the sake of his future. They felt that one day he would understand.

Delavan

In the fall of 1927, at the age of 14, Abraham was sent to the state residential school for the deaf in Delavan, Wisconsin. Delavan is smaller than Fond du Lac and located in the southeastern part of the state. It was not unusual for schools for the deaf or "benevolent asylums," as they were called in the early years, to be located far away from metropolitan areas. The distance shielded the deaf students from an intolerant society and, in turn, society was protected from having to deal with a handicapped segment of its population.

When Abe arrived at the school he did not want to stay. He begged his parents to take him home and did not understand what he had done to deserve the punishment of being separated from his family, but Freda could not explain and left Delavan feeling guilty and sad. Abe was alone and frightened of this small community of deaf society, isolated from the world. Yet the children there seemed happy as they expressed their fast-flowing ideas through hand movements and facial expressions to others who seemed to understand the most subtle shades and meanings of their movements.

On the first day a tall and friendly young man, noticing Abe's bewilderment, introduced himself and immediately took on a self-assigned "protector" role. Harvey Boldt, who would later become Abe's first roommate, invited Abe to his dormitory room and along with the strange hand movements used his voice to slowly mouth the words of the English language. Abraham tried to read the words on his lips.

Harvey liked Abe immediately and in the following weeks would continue to talk slowly to Abe whenever he signed, so that Abe could begin to associate his new symbol system of Signs with the few English words that he already knew. Fast movements confused Abe and meant nothing to him in the beginning. In addition he had concluded erroneously that the students using Sign Language were not smart, and he did not wish to be associated with most of them. He did not understand that in addition to the signs, the students were forming individual letters of the alphabet on their hands, or "fingerspelling." This manual expression of English would become the key to his understanding of the English language. Fingerspelling would be his major method of English language communication in the years to come.

The first several months were exceedingly difficult for Abe. He was placed in a special class because of his poor English skills. He cursed his mother again and again for abandoning him in this strange place. He wanted to leave and never return.

He had his first opportunity to go home on Thanksgiving in 1927. When he arrived home he was clearly upset and complained that the school work was too simple. He complained that one of his textbooks was a book he had used two years before in his Fond du Lac school. His complaints were so intense and persistent that his mother was prompted to write a letter to Superintendent Bray asking that Abraham be moved to a more challenging class.

Following are excerpts of letters which were exchanged:

Letter to Mr. Bray (12/19/27):

I wonder how is Abraham getting along now? When he was home for Thanksgiving, he told me that the school work was very easy for him and I want to know if you could let him go to a higher grade. Please let me know soon.

Response to Mrs. Barash (12/28/27):

You asked me how Abraham is getting along in school, and stated that he told you at Thanksgiving time that his work is too easy for him. In checking this up I find that he is especially good in arithmetic, but he is behind in language and several other subjects. He takes things too easy and does not realize when he does not have his lesson. However, he is receiving just the training that he should have, and I feel that inside of two years you will notice a great change in him.

The following exchange of letters occurred shortly after the first:

Letter to Mr. Bray (1/5/28):

Received your letter and you wrote that Abraham is not satisfy then he don't have his lesson. This don't satisfy me either, because I want him to study hard and get more knowledge. Abraham told me that Abraham had the same books of what he had when he was in the third grade. I can't understand why you keep him back instead of going further . . . I have an awful hard time to make him go back to Delavan. Abraham always cry when I try to tell him that the school is good for him and I want him to go back. I told him that he will be a printer and he said that he want to try it out now and give him half an hour everyday in printing shop. Probably this will satisfy him. Otherwise it is no use to keep him there if he don't like it. There is a very good school in Fond du Lac for Abraham, but I want him to stay in Delavan on account to learn him a trade.

Response to Mrs. Barash (1/11/28):

I received your letter a few days ago with reference to your son, Abraham. I know that you want Abraham to get along as fast as possible and are doing the best you can for him, but you have no idea of Abraham's lack of knowledge in subjects that he should know. Abraham goes home to you and tells you that the work is so easy that he does not have to study, but his language is dreadfully poor. He cannot express himself in good English and this is because he has no foundation. He is a bright boy but many of the important subjects have been neglected, and his foundation is so poor that he has practically no ability to read even the simplest books.

We are trying to help Abraham along this line as much as possible, and we cannot put him in the printing department unless he masters the English language, and this he has failed to do. It is hard to impress upon him that he must go to the bottom and get things right, but if he is ever going to get anywhere that is what he will have to do. We will try Abraham the rest of the year, and if he does not make better progress than he has made so far we shall not recommend that he come back .

Abraham is a good boy, and he does not cause us any trouble, and he has the ability, if you will only be patient and help him and us to try to straighten him out.

Printing was a prestigious and popular trade for deaf individuals during those years, but it was a vocation that required good English skills. Abe had a double handicap. Not only was he unable to *hear* English, he had never seen it formed on the lips or printed on a page until he was well past the prime time for language acquisition.

During the following year additional letters were exchanged between the school and Abe's family regarding the young man's progress. He was eventually enrolled in the shoe repair program, despite his family's dream and his own dream of entering the printing field. A letter, written May 30, 1929, from Mr. Bray to Abe's mother reads in part:

> *With reference to your request for Abraham to take printing, I will say that we do not allow pupils to take printing until they have made a good record in English, and this seems to be Abraham's hardest subject so he will not be able to take printing. He is doing much better work in the shop than he did last year, and I am quite sure that he will be able to make a living when he completes the work in the shoe department.*

Within two years Abe had improved in school and in the shop. He had developed a reputation as the best student, the number one student, in shoe repair. Teachers marveled at his craftsmanship and many of the staff began to send their shoes to the school shop, specifically requesting that Abe do the work.

Gradually Abe became more comfortable using Sign Language. He found his new communication system useful for learning, and he discovered that he could also use it to tease. Although he was extremely shy and did not talk about girls, he never passed up an opportunity to tease the girls working in the kitchen. One of his favorite pastimes was to untie their apron strings as he walked by. Many of the young girls hoped to get the attention of this strong, handsome boy, but Abe had decided that his life now had a serious purpose. Harvey Boldt recalls that Abe had vowed to become the best shoe repairer he could be. He was beginning to achieve focus for the very first time.

Football

Abe's participation in the school's athletic program sharpened his cognitive skills as well as his athletic skills. He was a natural athlete and became seriously interested in football. He had experimented with baseball and wrestling, but football was his favorite sport. The rules of football had not been difficult to learn, and the coach had devised a way to differentiate each play and position for the players by the use of letters and numbers, all in Sign. Abe mastered these signals quickly and soon became a valuable member of the team. He played the position of tackle, and because of his strength and agility, was feared by the opposing linemen. He often demonstrated to his children later in life how he would crouch at the line, carefully watching the ball, and then as the center snapped it, he, along with the other linemen, would initiate the play.

The football team traveled throughout the Midwest for games against other schools and those travels enlarged Abe's world beyond Fond du Lac and Delavan. Suddenly Abe was riding the bus with his teammates, responding to peer pressure and participating in mischievous pranks for the first time. John Kuglitsch, the team quarterback and a close personal friend later in life, recalls that Abe would join him and some of the other players as they stole off to the downtown area seeking adventure. They sometimes smoked cigarettes and even got into minor scrapes with the law. John observed that Abe was never completely comfortable in those situations.

Jewish Identity

As Abe returned to Delavan year after year, the Jewish traditions so important to his family became less and less

Young Abe (first row, third from the right) on the Wisconsin School for the Deaf football team. He played tackle and was feared by the opposing linemen. The football team traveled throughout the Midwest and those travels enlarged Abe's world.

familiar to him. Although several other Jewish children attended the school, it was virtually impossible to maintain a Jewish identity. The school was a microcosm of the larger Christian society, and Abe was expected to become a part of it.

Freda Barash once wrote to Superintendent Bray asking that Abe be allowed to come home in the spring for Passover. Mr. Bray denied the request, explaining that no vacation was granted for Easter, either. In the fall, Freda again wrote, giving the dates of the Jewish Holy Days and asking him "not to let Abraham work on those days. Please let Abe have a good time." These were the poignant requests of a mother who felt helpless in the face of what she knew to be more important educational and vocational issues. It is probable that no special privileges were ever given, and as a result Abe lost all awareness of these Jewish holidays during his adolescent years. It was not until he married that his Jewish identity surfaced once again, because his wife, determined to have a Jewish home, encouraged Abe's participation in the rituals and traditions of Judaism.

School Activities

Although Abe's communication with his peers steadily improved, he found communicating with his family increasingly difficult. American Sign Language had given Abe an ease of communication with his schoolmates, but it was virtually useless with his family. At home, on his two school breaks during the year, he found mealtimes especially difficult. He was unable to participate in most of the conversation and like many deaf youngsters in hearing families, he began to feel left out and rejected. He found himself anxious to return to school where he could converse about a myriad of subjects.

Harvey Boldt continued to be Abe's mentor and friend. Often they would walk down to the small apple orchard near the school, pick as many apples as they could carry, and stuff themselves for the rest of the afternoon. Abe cherished those

All of the boys at the Wisconsin School for the Deaf were members of the Governor's Guards. Here Abe (left) is dressed in a special uniform designated for the Governor's Guards Memorial Day march.

Abe planting a tree in his horticulture class at the Wisconsin School for the Deaf. There were many opportunities for learning outside of the classroom.

moments of companionship. He became peripherally involved with the Boy Scouts, who met five times a year. In the spring the Scouts would take walks to Turtle Lake or go camping in the woods. Many of the boys worked on achieving various badges, and although Abe was not involved in that aspect of scouting, he seemed to enjoy the companionship.

All of the young men at the school were members of the Governor's Guards. The Wisconsin School for the Deaf, as a state school, was directly under the supervision of the state government. Each year on Memorial Day the deaf students dressed in the special uniforms designated for the Governor's Guards and marched to the cemetery in Delavan. They were all required to carry heavy guns from Civil War days. Each boy considered it an honor to be a part of this special unit, singled out by the governor of the state, and Abe was no exception. Years later, he proudly displayed a picture of himself as a Governor's Guard among the pictures on the wall of his shoe shop.

Shoe Repairing

As Abe neared the end of his schooling at Delavan, he spent more and more time in the shoe repair department. There was no doubt that Abe was the outstanding student in this area, and that he applied himself in a way that the other students could not match. It was not unusual for Abe to disappear for hours at a time to immerse himself in perfecting his skills. At times he was even excused from the special Saturday duties expected of the boys so that he could continue his shoe repair work.

During his seven years at the school, he had won the respect and admiration of both his classmates and teachers. In 1934, during Abe's last year there, Superintendent Bray, in response to a request for a letter of recommendation, wrote the following:

We find that Abraham's work here is of a very high type both in school and in our shoe shop. If someone would take a little interest in him and show him just what is to be done, I am sure he would comply with any reasonable requests. He is a young man of high moral character, and gets along very well with those with whom he works. He is eager to work, and is very painstaking, and I recommend him for any position that he is willing to accept.

In spite of his excellent work in the shoe repair area, Abe still was struggling to improve his English language skills. Harvey Boldt recalls that Abe often sat frustrated for hours in front of a dictionary, looking up simple words. From the time he entered the school with only a few English words until he departed, he attained only a fourth to fifth grade reading level. This amount of progress may seem meager, but considering his background, it was a remarkable achievement.

In 1934, Abraham turned 21 and left the Wisconsin School for the Deaf. He had completed his vocational training in shoe repairing, but did not receive a diploma from the regular academic program. He left as quietly as he came. He would be remembered by his classmates as extremely quiet and shy, yet ambitious and persevering. The boy had grown into manhood here. The school had trained him for a vocation and had provided him with a communication system and a language that would be his entry into the larger Deaf community.

Abraham Morris Barash was now equipped to take care of himself and perhaps, in the future, a wife and family. He never would have to become a ward of the state. Freda Barash's dream for her son had come to fruition and she would be forever grateful to the school's staff for helping Abe grow and develop. What she had not counted on was that he would continue growing and developing, eventually pushing her out of his life.

CHAPTER 3

COURTSHIP AND ENGAGEMENT

During Abe's last few years at Delavan, his visits home grew more and more stormy. His younger sister, Lucy, born in Fond du Lac in 1926, after the family had been reunited, remembers that her mother worried about Abe as he grew older:

> My mother worried a lot about him and would sit and talk to my father about what's to become of Abe, and what's to happen and what's to occur. As he grew to be fifteen, sixteen, seventeen, and eighteen, Abe became restless. The world at that time was really kind of scary because jobs were hard to come by, the future was very unstable, people were really very poor, and there were a lot of homeless people.
>
> My mother and Abe began getting into arguments, because he wanted to drop out of school and he wanted to "go out into the world." He wanted to explore the world and my mother was so worried about that, because she was sure that's what he would do. He was so strong-headed. He said that he was going to go out and jump on a boxcar and travel all over the world, all over the country, that he was going to live like a hobo.

Freda believed that if Abraham were to meet an eligible Jewish girl, he might be more inclined to settle down. Accustomed as she was to planning out other people's lives, Freda actually placed ads in the *Jewish Forward,* a popular newspaper published in New York, seeking a deaf girl from a good Jewish family. It is not known if her ads were ever answered, but she devoted great energy to finding a wife for Abe.

Hilda Nathenson

In early 1934, Freda learned about Hilda Nathenson, a beautiful deaf girl of Russian Jewish descent in Madison. The daughter of Tilly and Meyer Nathenson, Hilda was nineteen and about to enter twelfth grade at Madison Central High School. She was a lovely, diminutive young woman, whose background was remarkably similar to Abe's in many

Although Hilda (upper left) had a severe hearing loss, it had occurred in early childhood after some normal speech and language had developed. Also note Hilda's sisters, Rose (far right) and Rebecca (upper right), as young girls in Russia. The other three children are Russian cousins.

ways. At age eight, she too had emigrated to the United States from the Kiev area in Russia, and she had been raised in a traditional Jewish home with strong Jewish values. Her father was a peddler and she had two sisters, Rose and Rebecca. The two families saw a nearly perfect match. On the surface, it would appear that the match had been arranged "in heaven."

There were differences, however, which later would prove to be significant. Although Hilda had had a severe hearing loss in early childhood, it occurred later than Abe's, and after normal speech and language had developed. In contrast to Abe this enabled Hilda to become much more successful with both spoken and written English. She had been integrated into hearing classes at Central High wherever possible and was an exceptionally good lip reader. The use of Sign Language in any form had been discouraged, and those who used it ridiculed, so that Hilda initially had very little ability to communicate in the very language that Abe knew best.

In addition, the childhoods they experienced, once they had arrived in this country, differed greatly. At the young age of ten, Abe had moved out of the family selling newspapers and working at odd jobs. He had been separated from his family when he entered a residential boarding school at the young age of fourteen. Hilda, the youngest of three sisters and handicapped, had been the protected "baby" in her family. She had been relatively sheltered and had not yet ventured beyond her family's doors. Abe had developed and become independent while living within the Deaf community. Hilda's development had depended upon her ability to negotiate within the hearing community.

The Meeting

When Freda learned about Hilda, it wasn't surprising that she aggressively pursued a meeting. Hilda's eldest sister, Rose, had recently married into the Rabinovitz family from Sheboygan, the same family with whom Peter Barash had boarded many years earlier, before his own family had arrived from Russia. It was through this connection that the Barash family learned about Hilda and the Nathenson family learned about Abe.

The Fox River Valley June Ball, an annual "get together" for members of the Valley's Jewish communities, seemed an ideal setting for the meeting. After school was over in the spring of 1934, Hilda went to the Sheboygan home of Rose's in-laws for a vacation and agreed to attend the dance, where she knew she was to meet the handsome, deaf Jewish boy from Fond du Lac.

Abraham was initially reluctant and resisted the arranged meeting. He had always been shy around girls and furthermore had formed his own ideas about traveling and exploring. His plans did not include marriage. He understood that marriage would bring responsibilities and recognized this meeting as an attempt by his mother to tie him down. Not willing to admit to his shyness, he argued that he had no money to treat this girl. Eventually, however, Freda had her way and Abe agreed to the meeting.

The family had no car, so Sara Manis, a family friend, drove Freda and Abe to Sheboygan, while Peter remained home to care for Abe's eight-year-old sister, Lucille. They drove straight to the Rabinovitz home, and it was there that Abe first set eyes on the beautiful and lively Hilda Nathenson, who would eventually become his bride. After awkward introductions, the young couple was taken to the dance.

This first meeting consisted primarily of glances, gestures, and overly exaggerated mouth movements. Hilda could not sign at all and Abe could not speak well. By this time, however, he was able to lipread English when the words were not too difficult. He was able to watch Hilda's lovely mouth and piece together the important parts of the words she was forming. His speech was not intelligible except to those who were in close contact with him at home or school, but he tried to speak, using gestures and signs to accompany his deep, soft voice. Initially, communication was a struggle for both of them.

Freda, anxious to know more about Hilda, found it easy to talk with her, unlike her experience with her own son. She questioned Hilda about her family, the people she knew in Madison, and about the school she attended. Hilda answered her questions politely. Freda was impressed with Hilda's ability to make herself understood. She was so taken by this lovely girl that after the dance she immediately invited her to return to Fond du Lac to spend a few days at the Barash home. This invitation was irregular, because usually the woman's parents were the ones to make such an overture. At first, the Rabinovitz family was reluctant to agree, but again Freda prevailed, and Hilda packed her belongings for the two-hour drive from Sheboygan to Fond du Lac.

Lucille remembers waiting up as long as possible so she could hear about the meeting from her mother, but she finally went to bed when she couldn't keep her eyes open any longer. She recalls:

> At last my mother came home and it was late. She crawled into bed, and my dad said, *"Nu* (well), did you see the girl?" So my mother said, "Did I see her? I brought her with me!"
>
> And she was sleeping. Here was this young, beautiful woman and I was involved in all this excitement at that time. I don't know if this was something that was told to me or if I woke up and there she was sleeping with me ... it was just such an exciting time. She was so full of life and she was just a really nice person. Everybody loved her!

Hilda stayed for several days before returning to Madison, and Freda began to use her homemade sign for "marry" (bowing a violin) whenever Abe was present. Lucille recalls that Abe had conflicting feelings, at first being "entranced by this whole thing," but then "giving our mother a hard time about it." He felt out of control as Freda continued to make decisions about his life. He tried to convey his frustrations to her, but without success. The momentum had been established and it continued.

Courtship

Freda was clearly in charge, and her next move was to ask the Nathenson family if Abe could work in Madison during the summer, perhaps as an apprentice in a shoe repair shop. Abe began corresponding with Hilda, and not long afterwards he took a job as an apprentice without pay at the Blue Ribbon Shoe Repair shop located in Hill's Department Store in Madison. While he worked there, he lived with the Nathenson family.

Freda made other arrangements as well, and invited Hilda and her other sister, Rebecca, to Fond du Lac for a few weeks. Rebecca remembers:

> The reason I got involved was that Mrs. Barash, Abe's mother, asked that Hilda come there and stay for three weeks and of course it looked a bit irregular to my mother. We were surprised, since usually it's the woman's parents who make advances.

During their stay with the Barashes, both the Nathenson girls were surprised to find that Freda, unlike their own mother, was not permissive with her children and did not allow them or their guests to be idle in the house. After dinner no one was allowed to sit and converse until the combination stove was polished, the dishes washed, and the sink scrubbed. The control that Freda exercised in her home produced obedient children and an immaculate house, something that Abe and Hilda would later resent. Rebecca recalls:

> In our household, we were talkers and the dishes would stay for a while, and would not be done immediately. I mentioned that to Mrs. Barash. "Oh, no," she says, "You have to. They all know what to do."

And it reflected itself later on when Mrs. Barash said that Hilda is different, that my mother is very permissive.

During that summer Abe and Hilda grew to know each other much better, and the relationship flourished. Of course, disagreements inevitably occurred along with a growing deep affection for each other. Hilda remembers that they had a big argument after a few months: "Abe and me had big fight at end of summer. I told him to get out. He cried."

Abraham returned to Fond du Lac and continued to feel conflict about the relationship, but in September he went back to Madison with his parents for the Jewish High Holy Days. He brought a small diamond ring with him and asked Hilda to marry him. "Abe say, 'I'm sorry. I make mistake.' He gave me ring and cry. I don't know why."

The couple became engaged. We have no clear knowledge of the events that occurred after Abe returned to Fond du Lac before the proposal, and we can only surmise that Freda's insistence, together with Abe's love for Hilda, led him to the ultimate decision to ask her to marry him.

Abe had hoped to return to Delavan in the fall, and Hilda had one more year to finish at Central High School. The plan had been for them to continue their schooling, but Abe decided instead to take a job in Fond du Lac. He had learned enough during the preceding summer to get a job repairing shoes at the Fond du Lac Dry Goods Store, where he earned eight dollars a week. During the fall months, Abe and Hilda traveled back and forth to see each other on weekends. Sometimes Abe took his sister Lucille with him as she loved visiting Madison and spending time with Hilda's family, especially with Rebecca.

Abe's job was a good one and his employer liked him and often joked with him, recognizing his good sense of humor. He respected Abe's knowledge and skill in shoe repairing, but by November Abe was laid off due to a lack of business. The shoe repair trade is seasonal in the Midwest, as

Abe and his fiancée, Hilda, during the courtship period in 1934. Hilda had designed and made the dress herself.

people wear snow boots and walk less in the winter. Abe was rehired for two weeks in late December while the regular shoe repairman was on Christmas vacation, but was then told to call again in the spring.

Without a job Abe became restless and worried and there was concern about what he would do while Hilda was completing her senior year in school in Madison. Freda encouraged an earlier marriage which would mean that Hilda would not finish her final semester, but the families could not agree about what should be done. Rebecca remembers being strongly against this plan:

> When Hilda decided to get married . . . it was very important in my eyes, and even her mother's, that she should struggle through and get her diploma.

Lucille, being only nine, was too young to participate in any discussions at that time, but she now reflects on the problem:

> My mother was very concerned that if Abe was not anchored, he might do something that would be in her eyes destructive, that he would go off, and wouldn't amount to anything.
>
> Neither of them ever graduated. I know, considering how much my mother valued education, that somehow it was very important for her that they get married. And I think it was probably even important for the Nathensons too.

Hilda, it seems, was more eager to marry than to work for a diploma. School was difficult, and the prospect of marriage much more exciting. Furthermore, her family was afraid that she might never be able to find another eligible Jewish man who was deaf. At Central High School Hilda had dated some deaf boys who were not Jewish. This angered her father, who insisted that she socialize only with Jewish boys and actually threatened physical punishment if she did not comply. Thus, it was decided that the marriage would take place on February 24, 1935.

Freda's rationale for encouraging an earlier marriage had been that Abe then would be able to start his own shoe repair business, using wedding gifts from friends and family to rent a shop and buy machinery. Without the marriage as an impetus, it was unlikely that he could ever do this on his own.

It was proposed that each family redeem similar insurance policies that they owned, on which they had been paying twenty-five cents a week. It was a common practice among families at that time to own such policies and they were worth about three hundred dollars each.

At this point, according to Hilda, an argument erupted between the families over money, expenses for the wedding, and who would pay for what. Eventually it was agreed that the Nathenson family would redeem their insurance policy and contribute $300, and the Barash family would provide the store situated at the front of their home, plus room and board, for one year. This arrangement had the potential for significant misunderstandings, considering the problems of communication and the question of how Abe's earnings would be managed.

The Wedding Ceremony

Although Abe and Hilda both came from traditional Jewish families, Jewish Law regarding the deaf in 1935 was still vague and there was a question as to whether they would be allowed to be married in the synagogue. Ancient Jewish Law forbade the participation of deaf mutes in contractual arrangements or as witnesses to legal transactions, because they lacked spoken language. Abe had not had a Bar Mitzvah and neither he nor Hilda could read or speak Hebrew. The decision was made that the marriage ceremony should not be held in the synagogue, but instead in the more secular Workman's Circle Building, where Hebrew was taught and Zionist meetings were held.

George Sullivan, Abe's good friend from Oshkosh, had a car and he drove the Barash family to Madison the night before the wedding. They stayed at the Nathensons' two-bedroom flat on Milton Street and early next morning, on the day of the wedding, snow began to fall. Lucille remembers:

> It had started to snow and it snowed and it snowed and it snowed. Your grandmother did all kinds of cooking, and she had many other women coming to help with the dinner.

Mrs. Lieberman, Tilly Nathenson's best friend, cooked for much of the day and prepared the chicken dinner to be served to the relatives before the wedding. Tilly made wonderful sponge cakes for dessert.

After dinner the wedding ceremony began. Hilda looked beautiful in her wedding dress purchased at the Cinderella Shop in Madison. She wore a veil borrowed from her cousin, Clara Cohen. Lillian, Abe's older sister, was the maid of honor and Hilda's eldest sister, Rose, was among her attendants. Abe's younger sister Lucille was the flower girl. She describes the wedding as "especially exciting, because I was a flower girl. I had never been to a wedding before."

Thirty family members attended the ceremony and dinner and sixty guests came afterwards for the reception and dance. Only a few of their deaf friends had been invited. Mr. Bray, the Superintendent at Delavan, had been invited, but had to decline:

> *I received the invitation to Abe's wedding to be held in Madison on Sunday, February 24th, and both Mrs. Bray and I would be more than pleased to attend if it was possible for us to do so. I am sorry to say that there is so much work at the school at this time of the year that I will not be able to get away.*

The day had dawned bright and cold, and by the

47

Abraham and Hilda on their wedding day, February 24, 1935, at the Workman's Circle in Madison. They marched down the aisle to a musical interlude they could not hear and watched Rabbi Cashdan as he silently moved his lips, not understanding the vows being spoken nor the hopeful and inspiring words. Interpreters for the deaf were unheard of in the 1930s.

middle of the afternoon huge snowflakes had laid a thick white carpet, making this special day in the lives of Abe and Hilda even more beautiful. The guests gathered quietly and whispered among themselves about the handsome couple and the good fortune that had brought them together. The match seemed perfect.

The procession began and Abraham and Hilda marched down the aisle to a musical interlude they could not hear. Their bright eyes shone as they watched Rabbi Cashdan, his lips moving silently, recite the traditional seven blessings and pronounce them man and wife. They did not understand the vows being spoken; they did not hear the inspiring and hopeful words. Interpreters for the deaf were unheard of in the 1930s, as Sign Language was not accepted or respected as a form of communication by the general public. Nonetheless, Abraham and Hilda seemed radiant in their happiness.

The snow continued to fall as the guests savored the tasty homemade desserts and danced to the musical strains of a small orchestra. Abe and Hilda made a beautiful couple as they danced to the beat of the vibrations they felt on the wooden dance floor. By the time the celebration was over the snow had become very deep and many people could not make their way home. What had started as a beautiful carpet of snow became the worst blizzard in four years, with drifts as high as ten feet and gale-like winds of over thirty miles per hour.

After they left the reception, Abe carried Hilda as far as he could in the deep snow, but when he finally tired, he put her down and they trudged through the blizzard, arriving at the family's Milton Street apartment wet and completely exhausted.

The storm continued through the night and newspapers describing the storm on February 24 reported buses stranded at farmhouses on their way to Madison. A sick child with pneumonia had been carried by sled from one of the buses to a Madison hospital. The highways were impassable and trains were not running, so the out-of-town wedding guests were stranded in Madison. They stayed overnight at the homes of family and friends, sleeping on cots or on the floor.

Hilda recalls that their wedding bed was given to a sick relative from Milwaukee. On their wedding night, Hilda slept on the floor along with many of the guests and Abe sat up on a chair next to her. They were unable to be alone to share their love and thoughts about the silent ceremony that had bonded them together forever. Hilda describes Abe as being very shy and uncomfortable with so many people around them. He spoke very little. The next day different arrangements were made and Abe and Hilda were given a room for themselves.

The out-of-town relatives and friends could not leave for three days until the highways were cleared and trains were running again. The young newlyweds remained in Madison for a few weeks before traveling to Fond du Lac where they would make their new home.

The Wisconsin State Journal

City, State, Struggle Under Raging Blizzard's Record Snow; Five Below Due Here Tuesday

Season's Heaviest Snow Provides Jobs for Men, Fun for Children, Trouble for Motorists

What started as a beautiful carpet of snow became the worse blizzard in four years with drifts as high as ten feet and gale-like winds over 30 miles per hour. This front page clip from February 25, 1935, documents the severity of the storm that occurred on Abe and Hilda's wedding day.

CHAPTER 4

STRUGGLE

The wedding brought together two attractive, Russian Jewish immigrants, both deaf. Born within one hundred miles of each other in Russia, they had been transplanted to the State of Wisconsin less than one hundred miles from each other in America. Both fathers had emigrated to the United States seven years before their families, and had worked hard to save enough money to buy passage for their families. Both mothers had shown great strength in caring for their families by themselves. Both families shared much the same attitudes about religion and education.

Yet, as similar as their backgrounds had been, the two young people differed markedly in their schooling once they reached this country. Abe had been profoundly and prelingually deaf when he entered Delavan at fourteen, but Hilda, having suffered her severe hearing loss in early childhood, had heard the sounds and syntax of a spoken language at a young age. She was sent to a Madison public school where she successfully learned to speak English and to understand the English spoken by others through lipreading. Abe, on the other hand, placed in an elementary class in Delavan with much younger children, reached only a fifth-grade reading level and continued to communicate mainly in Sign Language. His speech and English language skills were limited in

Meyer Nathenson, like Peter Barash, had emigrated to the United States seven years earlier than his family. As a young man in Russia he had been conscripted into the service of the Czar. Here he is shown in uniform before he went off to search for a new life in America.

Tilly and Meyer Nathenson, Hilda's parents, shown in a photograph taken while still in Russia before Hilda's father left for America.

comparison to Hilda's, but his awareness, powers of observation, and understanding were more developed.

Once settled in Wisconsin, their home lives had differed as well. Hilda had remained at home and was the baby of the family. In spite of family problems related to money and financial security, she felt loved and protected. Abe felt loved as well, but he had become more independent at an earlier age. By age ten he was out of the house peddling papers and earning money. At fourteen he had left home. He spent the rest of his growing years in a residential school, separated from his family and fending for himself without the love and warmth that he might have enjoyed at home. He traveled with the football team and developed a broader perspective of the world. Hilda, by comparison, had scarcely ventured away from home.

Early Misunderstanding

Abe opened his shoe repair shop in the store located in the front of the Barash home in Fond du Lac as had been decided. Freda, who had operated a small clothing store there since 1923, closed her store and turned it over to Abe. The store and living quarters were wedding presents from the Barashes, and the Nathenson family contributed three hundred dollars for the machinery. Abe and his mother traveled to the surrounding communities searching for used machinery. When the shop was ready, cards stating that he was new in town, was deaf, and was starting a shoe repair business were printed, and Abe walked door-to-door distributing them all over Fond du Lac. Unfortunately, an established shoe repair shop stood directly across the street in competition with Abe. This was during the Depression and business was very slow. For nearly a year Abe sat idly in his shop, attracting few customers and bringing in little money. He hated being idle and became restless. Relations soon became strained between the young couple as well as between the couple and Abe's parents since they all lived together in close quarters.

Abe quarreled often with his mother and he began to think about moving away from his competition across the street to Madison where he knew there were many university students and the possibility of more business.

The details of those family arguments are not clear. In years to come, we children came to believe that both the Barash and Nathenson families were devoted to the young couple and wanted to do whatever they could for them. Nevertheless, there were serious early misunderstandings.

As Abe and Hilda told it, business was poor with very little income. At first, some of Abe's deaf friends from the area came to visit; however, they soon stopped coming because Abe's mother asked them to leave when it got dark in order to save electricity. Freda also asked Abe for the little money that he did earn and she told Hilda that the Nathenson side of the family should be contributing more.

As the story goes, Hilda, due to her protected upbringing, was not used to doing housework in the way her mother-in-law expected; Abe's mother considered Hilda to be "delicate with delicate little hands," and didn't believe that Hilda would ever be able to do all the things that a housewife was expected to do. She accused Hilda of being a spendthrift, because she had once spent five cents on a mirror and some face powder. Abe was incensed by the accusation and reportedly went to Madison in a rage to discuss his plans for moving there. In his anger he tried to explain why he wanted to leave Fond du Lac, but he was finally persuaded to go back by the Nathensons. Hilda says now that she would have been afraid to leave with Abe, because she had been schooled carefully by the Nathenson family not to leave nor to urge Abe to leave so as to prevent her mother-in-law from saying later that the Nathensons had encouraged her to make trouble.

One night, a crucial conversation about night school provided the impetus for the move. Lucille recalls:

My mother saw that Abe and Hilda were sitting there in the house night after night and this was not good for them. So she said, "Why don't you go to night school?" And Abe said, "I can't afford it. I don't have the money." And she said, "It's just a dollar for the course. I'll give you the dollar." Abe blew up because he felt that she was offering him charity and he didn't want that. He would not take the money and he wouldn't go to school. They had a big fight and he packed up and went to Madison.

Hilda recalled that Abe resented this act of "charity" and angrily accused his mother of holding over eight hundred dollars of his newspaper earnings from him; it was money which he had turned over to her before going to Delavan. When he threatened to move to Madison, she laughed, saying, "You can't run away. You have no money and you can't take the machinery." With that, Abe went to Madison for the

Peter and Freda Barash at about the time Abe and Hilda moved to Madison. Freda said, "You can't run away. You have no money and you can't take the machinery." Peter privately favored the move and told them to go.

second time and demanded that Hilda's family help him. He wanted them to approve the move and help him move the machinery to Madison. When they refused, he threatened that he and Hilda would run away to Florida. He had threatened to run away before and the family believed he was capable of doing it, so they agreed to help him.

The next day he appeared in Fond du Lac with his father-in-law, his brother-in-law Bill, who was a lawyer, and a truck. He demanded the machinery and an insurance policy on which he had paid twenty-five cents a week and which was near maturity. Bill threatened a lawsuit and the related bad publicity. Mrs. Sadoff, a family friend, came to the house and intervened when she saw the truck, urging Freda to let them go. Freda released the machinery, gave him the insurance policy, and Abe and Hilda moved out.

Hilda remembers that Peter, Abe's father, had favored the move and privately told them to go, giving them whatever cash he could. Abe's younger sister, Lucy, was very sorry to see them go; although she was only nine, she recalls the day vividly:

> I can remember when they came with the truck and took the machinery and that was so devastating and so sad. Suddenly they were gone. I had liked having them there, because it was interesting and exciting. There was somebody else there, somebody else to talk to, somebody else to do things with, and somebody else to play with. I was always just very, very fond of Hilda because she was warm and friendly. During those days, I also learned a bit about shoe repairing. I worked with my brother. He would show me how to take the heels off and explain what all the machines did. I'd buff shoes for him too . . . but that was that. Then the Dark Ages descended, and it was sad. My mother was sad and depressed and very angry. There was no communication between them.

Move to Madison

When Abe and Hilda arrived in Madison, the members
of the Nathenson family were cautious, as they were afraid
that they would be accused of turning the young couple
against Abe's mother. They did not want to repeat the problems that had resulted from Abe and Hilda living with in-
laws, so they arranged for the young couple to live in a room
on the second floor with the Herman Onheiber family, friends
of the Nathensons. They were to pay rent, but Abe used to
help Mr. Onheiber unload fruit at the train station for two
hours every evening and Hilda thinks that the Onheibers may
have canceled the rent in exchange for his work. On the other
hand, she doesn't think Abe would have accepted compensa-
tion, as he was so grateful to be living in their home.

They had kitchen privileges in Mrs. Onheiber's strictly
kosher home, and Hilda remembers being criticized for frying meat in a pan intended for dairy foods. (Kosher dietary
laws prohibit the mixing of meat and milk products and
require separate pots, pans, dishes, and silverware for meat
and milk.)

Sam Onheiber, one of the sons, was six or seven years
younger than Abe and describes him as an extremely muscular and handsome man. Sam often went up to their room and
Abe proudly showed him the pictures of himself on the
football team at Delavan. Leonard Sweet, who visited his
grandmother there, communicated with Abe via notes and
recalls:

> Abe was a real good-looking guy and a big guy. I
> remember vividly that shock of black hair. . . a good-
> looking guy, smiling eyes, nice personality, always
> wanted to shake hands with you. When I shook hands
> with him, I couldn't get loose. He could break your
> arm off . . . He couldn't speak verbally, but he could
> sure understand people and he made his feelings well
> known. You could tell when you communicated with

The Herman Onheiber home located on Mound Street in the "Bush." The young couple lived in one room on the second floor when they first moved to Madison. Abe helped Mr. Onheiber unload fruit at the train station in the evenings.

him on paper, that he had deep feelings for people. And he was outward going. If he could have spoken, it would have been so much easier for him.

They searched for a shop and found a tiny Quonset hut, eight feet wide by fifteen feet deep, located near the University at 1107 1/2 Regent Street. It did not have running water or a bathroom, but Abe was happy with the location and rented it for ten dollars a month. He moved his machinery into the shop and began to wait for customers, but once again he had a slow start; he decided to distribute circulars door to door as he had done in Fond du Lac. He also gave delivery service to the students, riding his bike to fraternities, sororities, and rooming houses in the area. Peter Chortek, a neighbor who lived a block away on South Mills Street, recalls those early days clearly:

I remember [Abe] very well. He was a wonderful man, very warm. He used to deliver the shoes on his bicycle after they were done. I remember the ankle guard he wore to keep his pants from catching in the chain.

He was the first deaf person I ever knew. I met him when he first came from Delavan. He was about ten years older than I, but we kept up a friendship until I left Madison around 1950.

I enjoyed going to his shop to visit. We would "converse" by writing notes back and forth. If I didn't understand, he would try to form the word on his lips or write it again. He gave such a warm feeling.

Hilda found a job making paper boxes in a factory for a few weeks, but then was laid off because there wasn't enough work; it was during the Depression and times were hard. Later she began to help Abe in the shop, waiting on customers and sweeping the floor. Peter Chortek recollects seeing her there whenever Abe went out to deliver shoes or to do other errands.

During that first year in Madison Abe did not see his parents at all. Letters were sent back and forth between the families, with Rose doing most of the writing for the Nathensons, and Freda responding through the hand of Lucille, who recalls:

Rose was very verbal, very bright, and very, very vituperative . . . it was really very painful . . . she would write these letters . . . and my mother would answer her back, except my mother couldn't write. And so she would have me sit down and she would dictate and I would write these letters . . . so this exchange went back and forth and I don't know whatever happened to the letters, but I know they would come, and then they would be sort of like a soap opera. I mean, you could hardly wait until the next episode. And then my mother would take the letters apart, word for word : "... and what did she mean by that? Why didn't she do this or say that?" It gave my mother a chance to orate. She wouldn't just sit there and dictate; she would pace back and forth. "Now write that down! Now what did you write? Tell me!" It was really something. She would take the letter and answer each sentence. This went on and on. It seems like it was an awfully long time ... and then Abe would write and I don't know if Hilda wrote too, but there were always these angry kinds of letters, and why did you do this and why did you do that.

These hostilities continued, and when Hilda became pregnant with Eva in early 1936, the news was not shared with Abe's parents. Later Freda found out about the pregnancy indirectly and was hurt that she had not been told. By the time that Eva was born on September 22, 1936, however, there had been a reconciliation of sorts and the Fond du Lac contingent came to Madison to see the new baby.

Almost immediately both families began fighting again, this time over what the baby would be named. In the end, because of the hostility, Abe and Hilda rejected a name from either side of the family and selected "Eva," a "neutral" name that they both liked, which was easy to pronounce and lipread. Before Eva was born, Hilda and Abe had moved to a tiny apartment on Milton Street, a few blocks from the shop. They moved in anticipation of the new baby, because it would have been too crowded in one room at the Onheibers'. They lived on Milton Street for less than a year, until the house at 1113 Regent Street, two doors away from the shoe shop, was offered for sale in the summer of 1937.

Abe was encouraged by both families to buy the building which had three apartments, a large one on the first floor and two smaller ones upstairs. Abe, Hilda, and the baby could live downstairs, and instead of paying rent, he could earn income from the apartments and use the money to help pay off the mortgage.

Abe was nervous about taking on responsibility for the apartments and worried about making monthly mortgage payments. Lucille recalls:

> When Abe bought that first house, it was with great fear and trepidation, because he didn't know if he'd ever make the mortgage payments. You know, he was going to handle all of that. And these sums must sound very strange to you, but in those days people were working for seven dollars a week. That was their total income.

Abe had not yet established credit and had no assets, but by that time Hilda's parents had nearly paid off their own mortgage. The plan was for Hilda's mother to sign the mortgage papers and Abe would make the payments.

It was remarkable that he finally agreed to purchase the 1113 Regent Street property, especially since another shoe repairman, John Raymond, had recently opened a shop one block away on Regent Street. Abe had had one experience already with a competitor across the street in Fond du Lac, and he was infuriated by the thought of another shoe repairman nearby. John walked past Abe's shop every day on his way to work, and for years the sight of him passing by would cause Abe to become sullen and depressed. In Abe's mind this was an intentional act designed to aggravate him.

Babies

Although Abe and Hilda were concerned about making ends meet, the new baby was a source of great joy to them. They were happy that she was "hearing," but the relatives worried about how Abe and Hilda would manage and how Eva would learn to talk. No electronic devices were available at that time, but the new parents trained themselves to wake up regularly during the night to check on her because they couldn't hear her movements or her cries. Hilda placed the crib next to their bed and it was not unusual for her to fall asleep with her hand in the crib, so that she could feel Eva's movements as she slept.

Relatives came often to talk to Eva, hoping to provide her with words that could be imitated, but it was not the same as having hearing parents who could reinforce normal speech and language patterns all day long. Another complicating factor was that the grandparents and many of their friends who frequently came to visit spoke mostly broken English or Yiddish. In spite of this obvious language deprivation, Eva did learn to speak without a significant delay. When she entered kindergarten she received speech therapy, but only for a short time; whatever the problem, it took her no time at all to improve.

In the spring of 1938, when Eva was about eighteen months old, Hilda found a job as a typist at the United States Courthouse. She worked for the Department of Naturalization, typing information into blanks on different forms. She

Hilda's mother, Tilly, when she was well and able to help take care of Eva. A special relationship developed between the two. Later, Eva was a source of comfort to her blind grandmother.

enjoyed her work and was well accepted by her co-workers. Her income was an important supplement for the young family.

Abe, who was still not busy enough in the shop, helped to take care of Eva while Hilda was working. After she left for work at seven in the morning, Abe was responsible for dressing and feeding Eva. He took her to the shop with him (only two doors away) where she played until she was sleepy, and then he took her back to 1113 for her nap, walking back and forth to check on her often. He changed her diapers in the shop or at the house whenever necessary. Eva apparently was left alone during those naps, which is hard to believe, but Hilda definitely remembers the routine that way.

At noon Hilda's mother came to take care of Eva and stayed with her until Hilda came home from work. Mrs. Nathenson often took Eva to the Neighborhood House so that she could play with other children for a few hours every day. By the time that Eva was two, Abe and Hilda sensed that she seemed lonely and they felt she "needed someone to talk to."

After Hilda had worked at the courthouse for nearly a year, she learned that she was pregnant again after she fainted at work. She was taken from the courthouse to the doctor, who made the diagnosis.

She says now that she became pregnant "by accident" and that "Abe didn't tell me I was pregnant." When pushed for an explanation, she is unable to clarify it. Although they may have wanted more than one child Abe and Hilda were upset by the pregnancy because they were so poor. The income Hilda earned from her courthouse job would stop, and they would have to struggle even harder. Hilda had heard stories from her friends at the Deaf Club about how to stop a pregnancy. Following the advice she received, she began to take the hottest baths she could tolerate, but to no avail. The pregnancy continued and Hilda knew that eventually she would have to stop working. Two weeks before Harvey was born, she left her job.

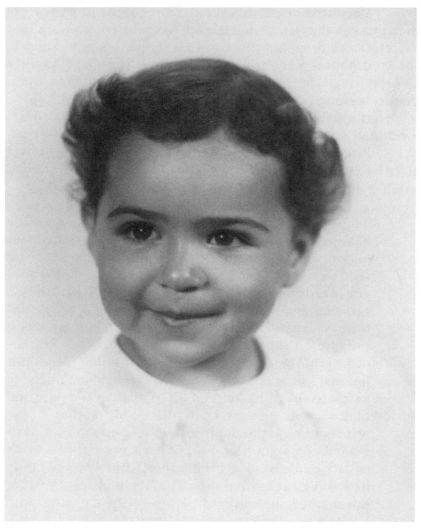

Eva, nearly age 3, awaiting the arrival of her new brother and "someone to talk to."

Very little discussion about babies or the birth process took place in the Barash household. As children, we were told that the stork brought babies, or that people bought babies at the courthouse. Eva recalls walking past the Dane County Courthouse, located near our grandparents' flat on West Main Street, looking into the basement windows. She was hoping to see the baby bassinets all lined up ready for purchase. Eventually, we learned something about sex from our peers.

Relations between the two families had improved after Eva was born, but many of the old problems resurfaced when Hilda became pregnant again. Lucille relates:

> The problems had kind of faded away, but then the hostilities arose again and there were some more complaints and arguments. And I think my mother and Hilda's mother liked arguments, because they would get into it with each other. They'd yell and they'd carry on and they seemed to be having a wonderful time . . . when Hilda was pregnant with Harvey, again they weren't speaking with each other. When Harvey was born Abe sent a telegram and it said, "Congratulations! We have a boy. The Bris (Jewish circumcision ceremony) will be held on . . . ." It gave the date and that was the telegram. I can still see my mother . . . she was standing at the ironing board . . . and she said, "His name is going to be Louie! That's my father's name and his name is going to be Louie!" But Abe and Hilda had some ideas of their own. My mother was very upset when she was told that the baby's name would be Harvey. However, she did put the name Louis in for the middle name.

Once again Abe and Hilda had resolved the problem by choosing a "neutral" name. It is not certain, but quite probable, that Abe chose that name because it was the name of his first friend and roommate at Delavan, Harvey Boldt, with whom he had lived for three years.

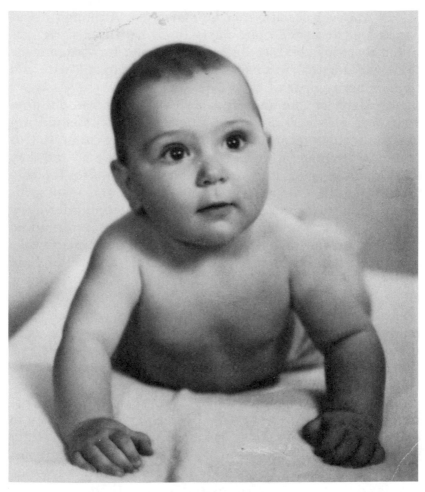

Abe was proud that he had a son who would carry his name forward. He handed out cigars to all his friends even though they were expensive.

Abe was ecstatic that he had a son. Although it was expensive, he handed out cigars to all his friends. He was proud that this child would carry his name forward, and he told everyone that Eva had "a baby brother to talk with and to keep her company."

Many of Abe and Hilda's deaf friends had children who were also hearing. Some had children who could not hear, and still others had both deaf and hearing children. Our parents were grateful that we both were "hearing," and they knew that they must provide frequent opportunities for us to learn to speak. Our relatives came to talk and read to us whenever they could, and as we lived only one door away from the shop, we went there often. The customers liked talking to us, and our parents were proud to show us off. Also, even though our mother's speech was distorted and pitched very high, we could understand her.

Our parents bought a radio for us to listen to in our home. They encouraged us to turn it on often and there is no doubt it reinforced our listening and speaking skills, even though we don't remember what we might have listened to.

We know that the tenants in the apartments at 1113 Regent Street spent time talking with us as well. Years later, after Harvey became an orthopedic surgeon, one of his patients told us that in 1940 a schoolteacher, who had lived in one of the apartments above us for a year, wrote a letter to her about us. She declared, "I hope to devote all my free time this year to teaching Eva and Harvey to speak." It is plain to see that in addition to our relatives and friends, there were many others who were interested in helping us learn how to talk. People did not realize then that hearing children of deaf parents do learn to speak eventually, some earlier than others, but most quite naturally.

Part II

CHILDREN —

A LINK TO THE

HEARING WORLD

CHAPTER 5

FORGING A FUTURE

Shoe Shop and Work

As the years progressed Abe gradually became busier in the shop, but he continued going door-to-door to pick up and deliver shoes. From the beginning his work was consistently excellent. His customers were happy and they kept coming back. He established a group of regular customers who were Madison residents in addition to the student trade that he generated by going to the fraternities and rooming houses. More students were moving into the neighborhood around the shop, which also helped.

The shop that Abe had rented from Mr. Barclay of the Madison Tile Company was small and cold, and there was no room for the machinery he needed. Mr. Barclay had agreed to sell the shop and the property to Abe when he retired and this time came about in the spring of 1940. Abe bought the forty by fifty-foot parcel and the three small buildings that stood on this property. There were two Quonset huts, one of which housed the shoe shop and the other a barber shop, and a tiny, dilapidated frame tile shop. After five long years of paying rent Abe finally began to make payments toward the purchase of his own shop. World War II had begun, and soon afterwards Abe got a second job at the Madison Kipp Defense Plant. He

Abe's tiny shop near the University at 1107-1/2 Regent Street. To drum up business, which was slow at first, he distributed circulars door to door.

worked twelve hours in the shoe shop during the day and another six hours at the defense plant at night, a total of eighteen hours a day. He continued this arduous schedule for three years until the war was over in 1945. In addition, he repaired army boots through a government contract and was proud to be a part of the war effort, since he could not enlist or be drafted due to his deafness.

The extra money Abe earned enabled him to pay off the shop mortgage in three and one-half years. He then proceeded to double its size by removing the rear wall and adding a new section onto the back of the building. In a larger shop, he had room for more machinery, so he traded his old finisher for a larger, more efficient one and finally purchased a Landis Stitcher, a machine he had dreamed of owning for years.

Abe with his new Landis Stitcher, doing his part for the war effort in 1944. Because of his deafness, he was not able to enlist.

Harvey: This large and powerful device, used for stitching leather soles onto heavy shoes and boots after the worn soles had been removed, made it unnecessary for this work to be done by hand. Although it would enable my dad to increase the speed of his work, the Landis frightened me. The huge curved needles were sharp and were driven with enormous force by the large machine parts so they cut easily through the thick leather. I watched my father in awe as he operated this machine, and the loud noise that it made when it was running at full speed terrified me. It was bolted to the floor and when its parts were moving, the floor shook underneath us, adding to my fright. I worried that my dad might damage his hands badly because the needles were stitching so fast that they were only a blur. One slip while they were cutting through the thick sole could spell disaster. I watched

This close-up of the Landis Stitcher shows the size and the power of the machine. When running at full speed, the large needles stitched so fast that they seemed a blur. One slip of the hand could spell disaster.

him for hours at a time through many years and he never once let on that he might be afraid. Instead, he looked at me out of the corner of his eye with a trace of a grin, reassuring me that all was well. In my father's skilled hands this machine meant that he could do more work and would be better able to forge a future for our family. He was beginning to believe in his ability to earn a living.

Making Ends Meet

In order to make ends meet, Abe's income from the shoe repair business was supplemented by renting part of our already crowded apartment. We lived in a four-room flat on the first floor of 1113 Regent Street and rented out one of those rooms. The rented room was situated conveniently at the front of the flat with a separate entrance. The kitchen, while small, was large enough to accommodate the table where we ate our meals. Our parents slept in the only bedroom, and the remaining room served as a living room during the day. The living room had a couch which opened into a bed for Eva at night. Harvey slept in a crib in our parents' bedroom and later on a rollaway bed in the middle of the kitchen.

Alice Walser, a deaf woman who was a little younger than Abe and Hilda, was our first roomer. She lived with us from 1940 to 1942. Alice had come to Madison from Freeport, Illinois, at the suggestion of Robert Horgen, one of Abe's deaf friends and the part-time director of the Wisconsin State Service Bureau. Mr. Horgen had advised Alice to leave the small town where she had grown up and come to Madison where she would meet a larger Deaf community. He introduced her to Abe and Hilda and it was agreed that she would rent a room in our home. The location was very convenient for her, as she had a job across the street at the Quality Laundry. Alice still has vivid memories of the time she spent as our boarder nearly fifty years ago. She remembers eating most of her meals at the table with the four of us. She recollects:

Hilda was an excellent cook. The food was delicious, although the portions were very small. Everyone was poor, very poor, but there was enough to eat.

Alice was a good baker herself, specializing in molasses, chocolate chip, and peanut butter cookies. We still remember the delicious smells of baking cookies wafting through the house on cold winter evenings.

Alice got along well with her "landlords" and remembers only a few disagreements between Abe and Hilda. "When Abe got angry, usually because there was not enough money, Hilda tried to calm him," she says. She relates that we lived in a bad neighborhood with few children. Alice does not recall that Abe spanked us; instead she describes him pointing a finger at Harvey and admonishing him, "Be a good boy . . . don't do it again . . . ask me before you go out to play."

She recounts how large the shop seemed after the expansion and how deaf friends loved to stop and talk with our dad. If he was busy, however, they would leave and come back another time. He worked very hard, often through the supper hour and on into the evening.

Abe and Hilda were very good to Alice. One year they gave her a surprise birthday party and she was thrilled, as she had never had a birthday party before. Hilda made most of our family's clothes and she made several beautiful dresses for Alice as well. Alice went with our parents to the Deaf Club, to picnics and friends' homes. Abe gave her advice about deaf suitors, telling her "to make friends with nice people," and she met her future husband while living with our parents. In 1942, she got a better job on the east side of town and moved out, but she came back often to visit. "Abe and Hilda were wonderful and really cared about me and I was not going to ignore them," she says.

In 1945 Merle Neefe, a hearing woman who also worked at Quality Laundry, moved in with her four-year-old daughter, Vicky. At that time she was in the midst of a divorce; the move to that room, and the relationship that she subse-

ber 10, 1940   MADISON · THE CAPITAL TIMES   WISCONSIN

The Sign Language Gets a Penny For Little Eva Barash

Lack of Ability to Speak and Hear Proves No Barrier to Happiness of Plucky Madison Man, Wife

By HAVENS WILBER
(Of The Capital Times Staff)

LITTLE EVA BARASH, who is 4, ran into her father's shoe repair shop at 1107 Regent st. one day last week. She reached her small hands above the counter and spelled out several words in the sign language of the deaf and dumb. Her father nodded. He went to the cash drawer, took out a penny and gave the coin to Eva.

A little later Eva was playing in front of the shop. She held a candy sucker in her hand.

Eva is the daughter of Abraham Barash, 26, who is deaf and dumb. His wife, Hilda, 24, is deaf. But these handicaps have not hindered the family in its effort to live normal lives. Eva, who is neither deaf nor dumb, has learned to communicate with her parents—to ask for pennies—although she is only 4. The couple has another child, Harvey Louis, 13 months, who has normal speech and hearing.

He Writes Answers

Barash explained by writing answers to written questions that he and Mrs. Barash, the former Hilda Nathenson of Madison, met through a friend, Mrs. Frieda Lieberman. About 3 years ago Barash lived at Fond du Lac with his parents at the [?].

"My wife was in Central high school here," Barash wrote in answer to a question. "A friend of mine, Mrs. Lieberman who lives here, saw her and told me about her. So I wrote a letter asking her (Hilda Nathenson) to come to Sheboygan for a dance. I said I desired to meet her there." Barash explained that he came to Madison to live shortly after-

ward, which was 5 years ago last Sunday. He said he and Mrs. Barash were married less than a year after they first met. He said his wife was the first girl he ever went with.

Born in Russia

Born in Russia, Barash came to the United States in 1922 and settled with his parents at Fond du Lac.

"Do you remember Russia?" Barash was asked.

"Yes, some," he wrote in answer. "I remember there were terrible times during the World war."

"Do you like the United States?"

"It's the best," he wrote.

Barash went to day school at Fond Lac from 1922 to 1927. Then he went to the Wisconsin School for the Deaf at Delavan where he learned the shoe repairing trade. He explained that Mrs. Barash learned the sign language from others who attended the Delavan school and taught in clubs for the deaf in Madison.

Barash explained that Eva learned the sign language from his wife. Mrs. Meyer Nathenson, 443 W. Main st., Eva's grandmother, is interested in talking with people in the shop every-

day," Barash wrote. "She is very talkative."

Speech Lost by Fever

Eva is in her father's shop very often during the day. The family lives nearby, at 1113 Regent st.

Barash lost his speech and hearing from scarlet fever at the age of 1. Mrs. Barash was deprived of her hearing at the age of 2, also because of scarlet fever.

When he started in the shoe repairing business in Madison, Barash explained, it was difficult to obtain business because of his lack of hearing and speech. Now after 5 years, Barash explained, he has a trade of regular customers.

A sign in the shop informs customers that Barash is deaf. The sign asks them to write their names and addresses on a tag, which Barash gives customers, and to check the items customers wished repaired.

Eva Barash, aged 4, (left) talks to her parents, Mr. and Mrs. Abraham Barash, 1113 Regent st. in the sign language of the deaf and dumb. Mr. Barash (right), who operates a shoe repair shop at 1107 Regent st., is deaf and dumb. Mrs. Barash (center) is deaf. Harvey, 13 mon the old son, is sitting on his mother's lap. Both Eva and Harvey have normal hearing and speech. Capital Times Photo.

This is a reprint of an article which appeared in the Capital Times *on November 10, 1940, the first of several articles to be written about Abe and his family.*

quently developed with our family helped to provide some stability in her life.

We remember her well, because we used to spend hours in her room talking. Her memories of living at "1113" are positive:

> Abe and Hilda were always so good to us . . . When I think of living in one room . . . we got along so well. There were times when I was behind on the rent, and they always understood . . . your parents took care of Vicky sometimes. I liked the porch. I sat out there so much. . . there was nothing bad at "1113."

She does not remember many children coming to play with us, but she clearly remembers one family around the corner who had children who swore all the time and who were a bad influence on us. She recalls Abe disciplining Harvey at age ten for "going with the wrong crowd."

She also remembers Hilda's parents being very ill:

> I could hear Hilda caring for them and I remember Abe shaving your grandfather's face. . . It wasn't a good time. I knew when both grandparents were dying. . . I remember locking up the house. . . I went to both funerals with your parents.

After Merle Neefe moved out of the small bedroom, Mr. Duncan, a man in his eighties, moved in to take her place. He has since passed away, but we will never forget the many beautiful animals he carved out of wood, the hours we spent playing checkers together, and the strong smell of pipe tobacco coming from his room.

In spite of Abe's added income from the defense plant, we were still very poor, and arguments over money continued. Abe was working over eighteen hours a day, and he was irritable and easily upset. In summer the unbearable heat beating down on the Quonset hut shop added to his discomfort and irritability.

Our house at 1113 Regent Street had its own woes. The storm sewers on Regent Street were inadequate to handle sudden large volumes of water during thunderstorms. Our basement was often flooded with water backing up through the floor drains. Abe would be in a very dark mood during the aftermath of a large downpour. He'd have to clean up the basement, which usually took several hours, after which a foul odor lingered for days. This happened at least three or four times every summer, sometimes more often. Whenever the basement flooded, the shop usually flooded as well. The water would rise over the curb on Regent Street, flow in under the door and even seep through the walls.

In the winter a coal-burning furnace and steam radiators heated our small home. Abe was responsible for shoveling the coal into the furnace and removing the ashes each day. He then had to carry the ashes out of the basement to the side of the building and later to the street. The heat throughout the building was regulated by the control knobs on each radiator and sometimes it became too hot on the second floor. Abe seethed whenever he saw the tenants who lived in the upstairs apartments open their windows to cool off, because he was paying good money for the heat that they were wasting.

A small wood-burning stove heated his shop. Mrs. Borsuk, who owned Borsuk's Grocery Store next door, gave him the wooden fruit boxes that were emptied each morning, and this wood, along with coal, provided the needed fuel for the day. Hilda remembers her own father often bringing sacks of coal in his truck for Abe after he returned from peddling fruit.

Without a Home

In 1945, when he was sixty-six, Hilda's father stopped bringing coal for Abe. He had had a stroke which left him paralyzed on one side. After the stroke he was no longer able to work and had trouble climbing the steep flight of stairs up to the family flat at 443 West Main Street. At the same time, Hilda's mother began to develop complications from diabetes and she was having trouble with her vision.

The families decided to switch flats in order to make life easier for Hilda's parents. We were living on the first floor of "1113" where there were only four steps to climb, so our family (Eva was nine and Harvey was six) moved to "443," and Hilda's parents moved into "1113." Most of the furniture in both flats was left in place, except for the rollaway and a few bureaus, making the move relatively easy. One of the benefits for us was the large RCA radio-victrola combination which was left behind at "443."

The move required that we transfer from Longfellow to Washington School, which meant that we had to leave many of our friends behind. Like most children, we had very little to say about the decision and we had no idea how long we would remain on West Main Street.

The worst result of the move was having to deal with the neighbors living in the flat across the hall. Two brothers and a sister, Tom, Ed, and Annie, and Annie's nephew Leo lived there. They were all heavy drinkers except for Annie. Leo had been a boxer at one time and was more or less permanently punch-drunk. They fought regularly among themselves and we often heard them brawling. We were not surprised whenever we found one of the brothers in a drunken stupor on the steps.

Eva: Even though they fought with each other, they never hurt us, although I was frightened when I was at home by myself. The worst times for me were during the winter when it got dark early, and I was alone for a few hours after school. My dad was usually working, my mom was at "1113" taking care of her parents, and my brother was in Hebrew School or at the Neighborhood House. I remember coming home, making a mad dash up the stairs, closing the door, and then locking it behind me with relief. One day I was sitting alone, reading. I heard a terrifying noise in the back bedroom and when I finally had the nerve to peek in there, I saw that it was only a shade that had rolled up suddenly. We had no phone and I was always worried about what to do in an emergency.

On weekends and sometimes during the day we went to visit Annie and even though we could smell the liquor in the apartment, we knew that she would be sober and we liked talking with her. She cooked and cared for her brothers and we often found her playing solitaire; sometimes she invited us to stay and play cards with her around the large dining room table.

On the days that I attended Hebrew School I walked the few short blocks to my dad's shop after class. While waiting for him to finish his work, I swept the wooden floor that never seemed to stay clean. It made me feel good to help him and the time passed more quickly. Spending time alone with my father was special. He worked long hours in the shop and in the defense plant, and more time was spent caring for the apartments.

After he finished fixing the last pair of shoes, and before the long walk back to 443 West Main, he began the daily routine of closing the shop. First he checked the machines by carefully touching each one, feeling for the vibration or warmth that let him know if it was running. Next he secured the back door and the window above it. He then turned off the main switch near the front door to disconnect the lights except for the bright red neon sign which made the words SHOE REPAIR glow brightly in the front window. Even though the electricity to run it cost money, he left it on all night because he thought it might prevent a thief from entering.

One more look around assured him that he had

completed his routine, and then, before stepping out into the cold, he put on his worn jacket, bundled me up, and closed the door behind him. The door had two locks on it. He selected the correct keys from his heavy key ring, double-locked the door, tried the door one more time to be sure that it was secure, and then we set out for what seemed to me like a long walk home. I felt warm and safe in the cold night air. He held my small hand, protecting me from the wind, and he looked at me often and smiled. Within a few minutes we approached a small cafe on the corner of Regent and Park called Bunkey's.

Bunkey's was one of my dad's favorite places, especially because it was cheap. He loved chili and could afford to buy a large bowl. On a cold night it was a welcome treat to sit at the polished counter and eat chili with my dad. I could order whatever I wanted. Everyone seemed to know him and I felt important explaining what people were saying. I had a chance to practice signing and to develop some confidence in myself.

After we finished, my dad gestured to me that it was time to go, bundled me up, and we were on our way again. When we arrived home, my mom was usually ready to serve a delicious hot dinner. We didn't want to hurt her feelings, so we never mentioned our trip to Bunkey's, and we forced ourselves to eat again, feeling a little guilty.

Our dad shoveled coal into the furnace at "443" in the morning before work and emptied the ashes at night. When he arrived at work, he repeated the furnace chore at "1113." In 1946, while we were living at "443," the furnace there was converted to oil, making his life a bit easier.

In the spring of 1946, the building located at 1111 Regent Street was listed for sale. That property was immediately east of "1113" and there was a shared driveway between the two buildings. Abe had had some problems with the people living at "1111" over the use of the driveway; sometimes strange cars blocked it. Purchasing the building would enable him to decide who parked there.

Abe had already paid off the mortgages at "1113" and at the shoe shop, so he was free of debt. Again he was reluctant to assume more apartment responsibilities and a new debt, yet buying the building made sense, and with Hilda's encouragement and both sets of parents favoring the idea, he made the decision to "go ahead." This time, however, he was able to obtain the mortgage in his own name, because now he had security "behind."

The layout of this new property was almost identical to that of "1113." There were two small apartments upstairs with a shared bath between them, and a larger flat downstairs. This lower flat, however, had a large kitchen, but no front bedroom. As at "1113" the furnace burned coal, but at the new property, an automatic stoker fed the coal into the furnace and Abe only had to remove the ashes at night.

Hilda's parents gradually became more infirm and needed more care, so Abe and Hilda decided to move from "443" to the downstairs flat at 1111 Regent Street. There they would be perfectly situated between the shoe shop on one side and Hilda's parents on the other. This decision suited them, but the tenants then living in the "1111" flat would not comply. Earlier they had gotten along well with our parents, but with the decision to move, a huge controversy erupted. Our parents hired a lawyer and it was not until almost a year later in the summer of 1948, after litigation in Small Claims Court, that they finally won the right to move into their own building. Abe, unhappy that he had had to hire a lawyer and go to court, seemed to lose his temper more often.

Anger and Discipline

During the first half of his life, Abe often had prob-

1111 Regent Street (center). After nearly a year and litigation in Small Claims Court, our parents finally won the right to move into their own building. Note "1113" on the right and Abe's shop on the left. This was his gradually expanding "domain" from 1936 until 1951 when our family moved to the west side.

lems controlling his outbursts of anger. Our mother recalls that when he was young, "Abe had a bad temper," but that in later years he "improved much."

As children, we clearly remember his angry outbursts and they terrified us. We could often read his mood in his face and in his eyes. In our childlike way, we would try to calm him and at times we were mildly successful. We had to be extremely careful with our own gestures and facial movements so that they wouldn't be misinterpreted. If we could not quiet him, he would often become more upset and suddenly he would explode, yelling in a piercing, high-pitched voice. We recognized the words he was speaking, but to others the sounds were unintelligible. When his anger reached this level there was no way to calm him. He once became so angry that he smashed a stack of dishes on the floor; the sight of the pieces scattered everywhere on the kitchen floor is burned in our memories forever.

He became angry at events beyond his control. Financial problems or basement floods upset him. He felt easily snubbed if hearing people were conversing among themselves and ignoring him. Since he couldn't hear what was being said, he often suspected that they were talking about or laughing at him. "Why they say bad things about me? They think I am low." He would push his finger up against his nose and say, "They stuck noses!" meaning they were stuck up. Sometimes his perception was correct and people *were* saying something hostile, perhaps making fun of his deafness, or calling him "deaf and dumb," or "dirty Jew." His own mother could easily anger him by excluding him from her conversation. She sometimes sat with us and explained her version of the early fights with him; he could sense what she was saying and would become very upset, shouting angrily, "Tell them the truth. Stop telling lies!" We know he felt vulnerable and unable to defend himself with words at those moments.

After these outbursts, he would often leave the house. At first we chased after him, pleading with him to return, but we soon learned that it was better to leave him alone; sometimes he would be gone for three or four hours, but he always came back. If ever we thought he might be unstable, it was at times like this. When he returned, however, we all cried, hugged and kissed one another, and then a long discussion ensued. We spent hours reminding him that he was a "rock," a special and hardworking father, because of the way he helped to lift us and guide us as we were growing up. Finally, fatigued from the emotional strain, we all went to bed, sometimes as late as two or three in the morning.

Most of these outbursts did not occur in public, but once, when two children in the neighborhood pushed their faces against the front window of the shoe shop with their thumbs in their ears wiggling their fingers, our dad stormed out of the shop, hollering at them in a high-pitched falsetto voice. He could also lose control if cars were left for many hours in the two-hour zone in front of his shop. He wanted these spots to be open for his customers, so he would wait at the window and watch for a violator to return. When Abe saw him he would run out, waving his fist in the air, and shout angrily, "You no obey the law! I will call police!" Harvey never will forget an argument between Abe and a neighbor in the small backyard of "443," having to do with the location of the property line and the position of some garbage cans . Abe, out of control and yelling loudly, embarrassed Harvey as more and more neighbors came to their windows. Harvey tried to stop the argument, but being only seven, he was pushed aside.

Occasionally our mother had trouble understanding Abe, because her Sign was poorer than his. If he was in a bad mood, he might become upset if she asked him to repeat what he had signed. He would become terribly defensive about his inability to communicate and would say, "She can't understand. I have to explain over and over." When these quarrels continued unchecked, both of them would end up regretting that they had ever married. Abe would say that he was tied down and had never been free, declaring that he could have graduated from Delavan and gone to Gallaudet College. Likewise, Hilda would complain that she should have gone on to college to study bacteriology. They both blamed their parents for "forcing us to get married." While Abe sometimes expressed great anger, we never saw him strike our mother. He vented his anger by yelling, running away, threatening injury to himself, and occasionally breaking objects like dishes. If he became upset with us, however, he was capable of giving a very hard spanking. He could administer this with or without the "belt." We developed a healthy respect for the belt, and just the suggestion that he might use it was enough to keep us in line.

> **Harvey:** When I was about seven years old, my dad caught me stealing thirty cents from the wooden drawer where he kept change in the shop. Stealing money from one's father was not to be taken lightly, and he gave me a royal whipping while he held me upside

down by my ankles. I never stole from him again.

In fourth grade, I brought home several notes indicating that I was disrupting the class because I "talked too much." This upset my father, but he did not spank me. A few months later the principal, Mr. Hargraves, sent a letter through the mail requesting a conference because there was still a problem. My behavior improved dramatically after a "teaching" session in the garage with my dad.

Eva vividly remembers breaking a glass dish filled with butter while reaching for cookies on top of the refrigerator. Butter was expensive. Although she doesn't recall being spanked at the time, she was extremely frightened by what our dad might do if he discovered the waste of butter and broken glass.

Although our father was a firm disciplinarian, we always knew that we were loved because he was more often warm and tender with us. We know now that he disciplined us physically because he didn't have the words he needed to do it any other way. Neither he nor we had the ability to verbalize our problems adequately. Harsh as the spankings might have appeared, they were his way of speaking to us and communicating his values.

CHAPTER 6

LOOKING OUTWARD

Willard Calkins was our parents' best friend in the Deaf community throughout most of the 1940s and early '50s. He was a large, round man who was always very kind to us children. Willard was good with his hands and sometimes helped Abe with repairs in the apartments. He liked to do carpentry work and we remember well the summer he built a new floor in our dad's shop in a matter of days. Abe never wanted to close the shop for even a day, so one weekend he and Willard moved all the heavy machinery to one part of the shop. Together they ripped out the floor and Willard quickly began building the floor joists and then the floor itself. When a large enough portion was completed, they moved the machines, and the rest of the floor was laid. Abe was pleased and Willard was proud of his workmanship. Abe insisted vehemently on paying for the work and materials, but knowing Willard, we're sure that the price was more than reasonable.

Since deaf people could not communicate by phone at that time, they met face-to-face whenever possible. Willard owned a car and on weekends he often drove us out to visit the Leon Elmer family or the Willard Sharer family at their farms. We usually spent the whole day, and while the adults talked, we played with the children.

On other weekends he took us to picnics. Over the

Abe (with hat) and Harvey (next to Abe) visiting the Leon Elmer family farm on weekends. Willard often drove us to visit deaf friends.

The young Barash family and Willard attending a picnic. Picnics, an important part of deaf culture, were a favorite way for deaf people to come together for hours on end. From front to back on the right are Willard, Abe, Harvey, and Hilda. Eva is in the front on the left.

years, picnics had become an integral part of deaf culture; even some of the signs for the word "picnic" conveyed the concept of conversation as well as the concepts of food and eating. It was perhaps the favorite way for deaf people to come together. When we were young, we eagerly looked forward to these outings, as food was plentiful and games and races of all kinds were planned for the children. Abe liked pitching horseshoes and sometimes joined in a softball game. Mostly, though, he just enjoyed signing for hours with friends. These picnics usually lasted until after dark when Willard would pile us into his car for the tired journey home.

Abe and Willard jointly purchased a toboggan, and stored it in the basement at 1113 Regent Street. When the winter weather was right, Willard would come to pick us up and with the toboggan on top of the car, we headed for the toboggan run at Hoyt Park. We spent whole days climbing up the hill and whizzing down the icy slide. The toboggan held eight, so sometimes we brought our friends along for a day of fun. Willard remained a close friend to our parents for many years. When he moved to California in 1952, he took Hilda and Harvey with him in his car to visit Hilda's sister Rose.

Robert Horgen and his wife Lola moved to Madison in 1936, one year after our father moved there. Both Abe and Robert had attended the State School for the Deaf together, but while there had known each other only slightly. Robert, five years older than Abe, had pursued a course far different from Abe. Because he was post-lingually deaf, Robert had wonderful language skills and he became an avid reader. After leaving Delavan he had gone on to Gallaudet College, the only college in the United States for deaf students, where he majored in English. There he met his wife, also post-lingually deaf, and the two were married after graduation. Not long afterwards they moved to Madison.

Robert was hired as a printer by Madison Newspapers, and in addition, worked part-time as Director of the Service Bureau, a state agency created to help people with problems specifically related to deafness. He took an active interest in

Robert Horgen had pursued a course far different from Abe. He had wonderful language skills and became an avid reader. After leaving Delavan he had gone on to Gallaudet College where he majored in English.

many of the deaf in Wisconsin in those years, but his help was not always accepted, as his education seemed to separate him from the average deaf person. He took a special liking to Abe who, in turn, responded warmly to him. Abe recognized at once that Robert was indeed far more educated than himself and most of the other deaf people he knew.

The two wives also got along well, and the four became fast friends during the ensuing years. Robert and Lola often dropped into Abe's shop and the two couples frequently visited each other's homes. Abe and Hilda considered it a high compliment that this "well educated" deaf couple wanted to pursue a friendship with them. The Horgens had no children of their own and they enjoyed the family life that they found at the Barashes. They did own a large dog to whom they ministered lovingly, taking him with them wherever they went. That dog is very much an integral part of our image of the Horgens in the 1940s. As they loved animals, they sometimes sheltered strays. Lola recalls a stray cat that they found in their neighborhood; she looked for someone to take it, asking many of her friends, but all refused except for Abe who offered to keep the cat in his shop. We don't remember the cat, as we were too young, but Lola tells us that

the cat was in Abe's shop for more than a year until one day
it disappeared — she thinks it might have been run over by a
car.

As part of his job with the State Service Bureau, "Mr.
Horgen" (as we were taught to address him) did our parents'
income tax forms for them through the 1940s until Harvey
took over in 1951.

> **Harvey:** These tax forms were very difficult for my
> dad to understand because of the language and the
> many pages and numerous blanks to complete. The
> work was easy for Mr. Horgen at first, but through the
> years it became much more complicated due to my
> dad's increasing business transactions, especially as
> they related to his income properties at 1111 and 1113
> Regent Street. They spent long hours sitting at the
> table organizing the bills, checks, stubs, and miscella-
> neous receipts.
>
> My dad knew that Mr. Horgen devoted much
> more time to this work than was intended by the
> Service Bureau, and insisted on paying him for his
> help. Forever the gentleman, Mr. Horgen adamantly
> refused to take the money, but finally accepted a
> token "tip," as my dad called it, just to appease him.
> I only watched at first, but I helped more each year,
> first organizing the many papers of all shapes and
> sizes, then later beginning to fill in the simpler blanks.
> By the time I took over in the early 1950s I was able to
> do most of the work, except for the problems con-
> nected with depreciation and amortization, concepts
> that baffled me (and still do). I felt free to call on my
> parents' good friend Mr. Horgen whenever I needed
> help.

Fond du Lac

Friendships within the Deaf community continued to

form our parents' most important and satisfying relation-
ships, but as the years passed and we grew older, relations
with our dad's parents gradually improved. Occasionally our
grandparents came to Madison to visit, but most of the time
we went to Fond du Lac by bus. Our whole family would go
for a weekend, for the High Holy Days, or for a Passover
Seder. The trips were fun, unless a fight ensued. In contrast
to the early days, the feuding parties usually made up after a
short time without carrying a grudge lasting for months or
years.

We children often went to Fond du Lac for summer
vacations. When we were younger, we sometimes spent the
entire summer there, so that we might be surrounded by
"normal" speech, although our grandparents' broken En-
glish-Yiddish was hardly normal. During several of those
summers we developed contagious diseases. Children were
quarantined when they had these diseases, and a sign had to
be posted on the building. Lucille recalls:

> I remember those wonderful summers when you
> (Harvey and Eva) came to visit. They were all so
> highlighted. It seemed like you got many of your
> contagious diseases in Fond du Lac . . . there was the
> summer that the kids got whooping cough. Those
> were the days before vaccinations. When you got any
> of these contagious diseases, quarantine signs went up
> on the houses. They said either "Quarantine" or
> "Chicken Pox" . . . but since there was a business, my
> mother couldn't afford to have a quarantine sign on
> her store . . . we lived in back of the store . . . and so this
> was all a big secret. Whooping cough in those days was
> a six-week proposition. I mean, you whooped for six
> weeks.

One summer, Eva got scarlet fever and was very sick.
Hilda had to come from Madison to help care for her. Our
parents were extremely worried, because the family sus-

pected that Hilda might have lost her hearing due to a complication from scarlet fever years earlier. Lucille recalls:

> Then there was the summer that Eva got scarlet fever, and your mother came to take care of her. . . Eva and your mother were kind of living in this bedroom in the back part of the store, and I would talk to Eva through the window. Fortunately there were no side effects, and she was okay.

As we grew older Abe's mother, Freda, invariably organized a summer work project for us when we came. The backyard was a mini-junkyard, because our grandfather was a junk peddler, collecting scrap metal which he often deposited in the large backyard while waiting for better prices. One summer, our job was to pull weeds and pick up nails and small pieces of metal from the property, for which we were paid five cents an hour. We worked all summer and during the last week, we took the whole family out for ice cream. We spent our entire summer's earnings at Petrie's Restaurant.

Going with our grandmother to auctions to buy used furniture for her store was a great adventure and always made us feel important. We would listen to the auctioneer's rapid clipped speech and marvel that he could be understood. Afterwards we helped load the truck, then unloaded it back at the store. She taught us how to strip, sand, and refinish the furniture, and later she taught us how to wait on customers until she came out from the family's living quarters in the back of the store. We sat in the front minding the store for hours amidst the ticking and irregular chiming of the many old clocks on display. We didn't feel exploited, because we knew she was teaching us, as she had taught Abe, to be industrious and not to waste time on "useless" activities. Besides, it was different and fun.

We sometimes went with our grandfather in his truck to collect scrap metal. We would get up at five o'clock, eat breakfast, and then leave for the country. We made the

Peter Barash, Abe's father, standing beside his truck. He made the rounds from farmhouse to farmhouse looking for scrap metal, rags, and other "junk."

rounds from farmhouse to farmhouse, looking for scrap metal, rags, and other "junk." Once in a while we hit the jackpot, uncovering a treasure-trove of items for which our grandfather had to pay only a few dollars and which would command big prices at the junk yard. At noon we ate the lunch we had packed for ourselves and we usually returned home by three or four in the afternoon. If we came home earlier, *Bobe* (Yiddish for grandmother) would complain that our *Zeide* (Yiddish for grandfather) was "lazy" and would lecture to us that she was shouldering all the responsibility in the family.

In later years, as we developed our own interests in Madison, our Fond du Lac vacations became shorter. Instead of going to Fond du Lac for a whole summer, we went for a month, and finally in the late 1940s, for only one or two weeks.

After returning from our Fond du Lac vacations, one of our annual late summer family activities involved pickling cucumbers and canning fruits and vegetables for the winter. Abe and Hilda had learned how to do this from their parents and we spent many weekends each year canning tomatoes, peaches, pears, applesauce, and making strawberry preserves.

Abe and Hilda studied the ads and then went looking for the best prices for fresh fruits and vegetables; sometimes they purchased bushels of produce directly from a farmer. If we were canning peaches, we would cut them up and boil them in large vats. At precisely the right moment, our dad poured the boiling water and fruit into canning jars, and then we sealed them with a cap and a rubber ring, and allowed them to cool. We often prepared as many as fifty jars at a time. These preserves remained delicious through the winter months and made wonderful gifts when we visited friends and relatives.

Sometimes we canned vegetables from our own garden. Abe enjoyed growing vegetables, especially tomatoes; we went with him to pick out the small plants and then helped place them in the soil. He beamed with happiness when his garden was "successful" and produced many tomatoes.

Our Aunt Lucy, Abe's younger sister, enrolled at the University of Wisconsin-Madison in 1944 and entered the medical school in 1947. After she married in 1948, she and her husband lived in one of the upstairs apartments at "1111." They were given the old family car, so on weekends we sometimes went to Fond du Lac with them, counting cows and playing Ghost and other word games in the car. As both Lucy and her husband were medical students, we learned the names of all the bones in the body on those trips.

Lucille received her medical degree in 1950. She specialized in pediatrics and later became a child psychiatrist. Abe was proud of his young sister, but again had reason to wonder how different his own life might have been if he had not lost his hearing.

Abe's sister, Lucille, graduated from medical school in 1951 and later became a child psychiatrist. While always proud of his young sister, Abe often wondered how different his life might have been had he not lost his hearing.

97

Harvey, 4, and Eva, 7, who were soon to become Abe and Hilda's link to the larger hearing world.

Radio

When Eva was born, our parents bought a radio hoping that she would learn from the voices she heard. They never seemed to resent the fact that we could hear the miraculous sounds coming from this box while they could not; rather, they encouraged us to tell them about what was happening in the world. As we grew older, we listened with the sound turned up as loudly as we wanted. We had no real idea about modulating the volume, and sometimes the tenants in the upstairs apartments would complain, asking us to please turn it down.

When we moved to West Main Street, we temporarily inherited an RCA radio-victrola from our grandparents. At first we listened to some of our grandfather's records, but we didn't care much for opera, which was his love. We preferred the radio. The set was quite large and stood on four tall legs; we liked to lie down on the floor and get in under the radio between the legs, where we could see the vacuum tubes and large speakers. We loved listening to different serials, including "The Thin Man," "Tom Mix," "Sky King," and "The Lone Ranger." "Fibber McGee and Molly" was a favorite as well.

Eva: At lunchtime or after school I would run home to listen to "Stella Dallas" or "One Man's Family," the original "soap operas." I loved learning about family life different from our own. It was exciting for me to imagine what each new episode might bring; I also learned a lot about the advantages of using Oxydol and Duz soap for washing clothes! Harvey and I liked "The Shadow" which kept us glued religiously to the radio. Later Harvey began listening to high school and UW basketball games and as the play-by-play came over the radio, I saw the beginnings of the "grunts, groans, whoops, and flailing arms" that can still be seen today whenever he gets caught up in a sports broadcast.

One of my favorite programs during the late '40s and early '50s featured fifteen minutes of Latin American music, and I loved to dance around the room imagining myself in the arms of a handsome Latino. My mom would come into the room and watch me dance, wondering what power music could have that made her young daughter so happy. I wanted her to share the beautiful sounds and rhythms with me, so I would turn up the radio as loud as I could and put her hand on the speaker, hoping that she would feel the vibrations. She responded, but always with a slight grimace, complaining that it hurt her ears.

Abe in the 1940s

Harvey: My dad had a large impressive trunk and upper arm muscles. I loved asking him to "make a muscle" and in response, he could make his biceps muscle as hard as a rock. Then he made it dance up and down by repetitively contracting and relaxing it. He could do fifty pushups on command. He could also do one-arm pushups, or stand on his head, or whatever I wanted. He made me laugh with his "monkey face" impersonation. To do this he tightened his thick lips around his teeth, closed his eyes, and flattened his upper eyelids against his eyes to make a monkey face and then scratched under his armpits with his long fingers, creating a real live monkey. I laughed at his impersonations, brought my friends over to watch, and made him repeat them again and again.

On Sunday mornings he did not have to get up early to work, so after sleeping "late" he would get up around nine o'clock, shave, read the paper, and then prepare for us his specialty, French toast. He performed this ritual almost every week for years, and no one, but no one, could make French toast the way my dad could. He had a special formula for the ratio of eggs to milk (later, water), knew precisely how much butter (later, margarine) to use to give the toast the proper glaze, and perfected the timing and rhythm of the actual frying, so that each batch was warm and ready at the moment we finished the preceding batch. He later taught me his recipe and technique, along with his incomparable recipe for pungent horseradish, and I promised him I would pass both on to the next generation.

My dad enjoyed "singing" while working in the shop. He called it "singing," although the sound he made in no way approached what most people would consider singing. He was able to produce a sound similar to that which a frog makes, far back in his throat. This sound was accompanied by a vibration which filled the neck and head when it was produced. I think that he considered this akin to music, because it produced a strong vibration like that which he felt when he laid his hand on a violin. He often "sang" with nails between his front teeth, feeding them into his hand one by one, as he nailed a heel onto a shoe. I admonished him for holding these nails in his mouth, warning him that he might swallow one or that he could get cancer from the metal, but he never heeded my advice.

Our father was living proof that clothes don't make the man. He showed no interest in clothing or fashion. He wore whatever clothes he had till he wore them out, and he managed to look good whether his clothes fit well or not. He dressed functionally, wearing flannel shirts, work pants, long underwear, and heavy boots during the winter; in the summer he wore a short-sleeved work shirt in the shop, and he often changed into a ribbed sleeveless undershirt at home. He was so handsome and his face so full of character that his choice of clothing didn't matter.

If he needed new clothes for a special occasion, our

mother would have to prod him to go shopping with her, and together they searched and compared values. Harold Sweet, who worked at the Capitol Tog Shop, frequently waited on them when they came into the store. He recalls:

> When your parents came into the clothing store, they looked for me. Your father would come up and tap me lightly on the shoulder. He was quiet and gentle, and he had a very warm smile. He and your mother liked to "feel" the material with their fingers before deciding. I always enjoyed taking care of them.

This act of feeling the merchandise continued through-out his life. Whenever we went shopping with him, we watched him handle the product and rub it with his fingers. He assessed the texture and quality of items ranging from shirts and blouses to curtains and rugs. He could tell the difference between a two-ply and four-ply rug by the feel alone. This ability carried over to leather products as well. When buying a leather purse or a pair of shoes he handled the leather, bending it in his hands, and then announced that the item was either "good quality" or "cheap." He also smelled the leather when making a decision; as we watched him work in the shop he often pushed a piece of leather up against our noses, whispering in his soft, guttural voice, "Good leather!"

His hands were huge and powerful. His fingers were long and thick, usually stained with shoe polish and machin-ery grease. His hands were proof of how hard he worked, and we could tell he was proud of them. They were beautiful hands, and we loved to watch them as he worked or as he "spoke."

He also "spoke" with his eyes. They were ever bright, shining, and expressive. Heavy eyebrows and long eyelashes framed and punctuated them.

He spoke with his heart as well. He was kind and generous, especially to people who were disadvantaged in some way. Mrs. Horgen, wife of his long-time friend Robert,

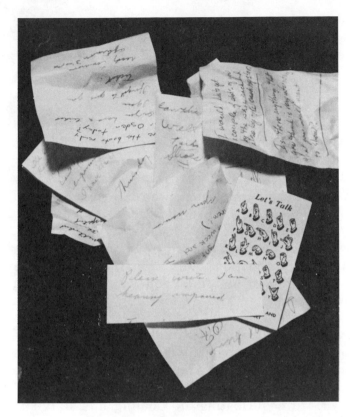

Abe loved to write notes with his customers. He often brought these notes home for us to read, so we would know what went on in the shop.

remarked that he was always willing to talk with and give advice to people whom others might consider to be of "low" intelligence without much education, people whom others might shun.

Bill Angel remembers bringing the wooden leg belonging to his amputee grandfather, John Parisi, into Abe's shop:

> My grandfather always said to take it to Barash . . . whenever I walked in there, Abe would drop what he was doing. I explained to him what needed repair, and he could look at it and see what was wrong. He would fix it up right away, because he knew my grandfather

was sitting at home without that wooden leg . . . and he always charged the same thing. It was always seventy-five cents, whether it was the heel on the shoe or the straps or anything.

While Abe was working in the shop during those years, he was in his glory. He was a king in his own castle. He loved to write notes back and forth with his customers, and he often brought these notes home for us to read, so we would know what had happened in the shop that day. People genuinely enjoyed his warmth. Mrs. Hoffman, whose husband owned the Hoffman Seed Company down the street, recalls:

> He was the sunniest, most happy person. I loved to go in and write notes and see his wide, broad smile. He was very skilled at his work. Your mother was often there, too.

Many people remember how hard he worked throughout his lifetime. This was especially true in the '40s — years of long hours in the shop and in the defense plant, of ever-increasing responsibilities for the properties at "1113," "443," and "1111." Mr. Miller of Heating and Cooling, now sixty-six, serviced all of these buildings from the early 1940s until Abe died. He remembers Abe breaking up wood for the wood-burning stove in his shop and later carrying oil back and forth from his one hundred-gallon drum behind "1111"; and he remembers Abe shoveling coal and removing ashes at each of the buildings. He sums it up simply: "Abe made that place go."

Hilda

During the 1940s, Hilda was kept busy helping Abraham in the shop and the apartments, caring for her parents, and raising her family. Peter Chortek describes her in the shop:

Abe and Hilda shown relaxing at a picnic. By 1940 Hilda's size eight wedding dress no longer fit and she could not lose the fifty pounds that she gained following her pregnancies.

She would take over when Abe went out to deliver shoes or go to buy leather. She would bring you kids with her and, as with any young kids, she had her hands full trying to keep you under control. As I remember, she was all business.

Most of her time during those years was taken up caring for our ailing grandmother, Tilly, who developed complications from her diabetes and needed frequent insulin shots. Hilda learned to test her mother's urine and was expert in giving her the shots, prompting others to remark that she should have been a nurse. She was very proud of these accomplishments, even though the responsibility was a heavy burden on her. Her mother gradually lost her eyesight and it became necessary for Hilda to do her shopping, to help her cook and clean, and to take her to visit her Jewish friends from the Old Country in the nearby "Bush."

Tilly did not make it easy. Frustrated by her life of

poverty and poor health, she became bitter and more demanding than in earlier years. Rose, Hilda's eldest sister, was occupied with her own family in Sheboygan, and Rebecca, the middle sister, had left Wisconsin and moved to New York. Hilda thus assumed the full responsibility for caring for her parents, and she accepted her lot with love and patience. She couldn't forget how helpful and encouraging her mother had been when she and Abe moved to Madison from Fond du Lac years earlier. Hilda was a good, obedient, and loving daughter. Even under difficult circumstances, she radiated love and sunshine, and she did not share Abe's frustration or unhappiness about being deaf.

Besides working hard to care for her parents, she was a devoted wife and mother. She had learned to sew as a child and made many of our clothes, as well as her own. She was a wonderful cook and baker, and we all loved eating her homemade bread, cinnamon rolls, cakes, pies, and cookies. Hilda could not resist them herself, and little by little she began to gain weight. By 1940 her size eight wedding dress no longer fit and she could not lose the fifty pounds she had gained following her pregnancies; her size eighteen dresses depressed her, but try as she might, she seemed unable to do anything about it.

Our mother loved to socialize and her deaf friends often came to visit. She and Abe were invited to a continuing round of deaf social events, including card parties, birthday

Eva and her friend, Annalee, in a Purim play. Because Annalee's parents did not work on the Sabbath, Eva requested our parents to be more observant, but her requests semed unreasonable. It was unthinkable for Abe to consider not working on Saturdays.

parties, showers, and picnics. In our younger years we usually went with them, but later we had things to do with our own friends.

Eva

Eva: I was becoming a young lady and making friends both at school and at Hebrew school. My best friend, Annalee Feigenblum, came from a very traditional Jewish family and I liked to stay overnight at her home on University Avenue near the campus.

Unlike my parents, Annalee's mother and father did not work on the Sabbath, and as I became a teenager I began to wonder about our family's religious practices. I wanted our family to be more observant and I talked with my parents about not working on Saturday and attending Sabbath morning services. I often went on Saturday afternoons to "Movie Club," which was organized by our rabbi to encourage the children to keep the Sabbath instead of going to the movies on Saturday afternoons. I also asked to be allowed, like Annalee, to stay home from school on the minor Jewish holidays, but my parents did not understand and refused. They had both come from traditional, but not necessarily religious, homes, and my requests seemed unreasonable. An education and the work ethic were much more important to them during those years. It was unthinkable for Abe to consider not working on Saturdays.

I did not understand my parents' reluctance and used the issue as a reason to rebel. I resented being asked to wash the floor or clean the porch on Saturdays; I much preferred being at Annalee's house, where we could spend the entire afternoon walking around the university campus.

As I look back, I feel that my parents expected a lot from me. Before I had even reached my teens I transacted business for them, making phone calls and negotiating with tenants. As Harvey grew older he helped me by sharing these duties and later he took over many of them.

In the summer I enjoyed going to Vilas Park with my friends, and sometimes I went with our family. People often stopped us to ask what nationality I was; I tanned so easily that I was often mistaken for Greek, Italian, or Spanish, or later, Israeli. My parents were very proud that so many people stopped to talk to them and admire their daughter with her dark, shining eyes, so much like her dad's. But my mother wished that I was not quite so shy. I would often hide rather than talk to people. I once saw my father reassure my mom in Sign that I would probably grow out of it, much as he had done. She was disappointed with my shyness, because she herself had been popular and attractive as a young girl and understandably wanted me to be the same way. Her expectations were to cause problems between us as I entered adolescence.

During these years I spent many hours with my *Bobe* Nathenson, as she needed more and more help because of her failing eyesight. We often walked together to the grocery store and to the fish market where she taught me how to pick out the best fruits and vegetables and how to ask for the freshest fish. Trips to Wisconsin General Hospital were commonplace as she spent more and more time doctoring for her ailments. During the endless hours in the hospital waiting rooms, I loved to read the funny papers to her. I proudly read aloud the books that I had taken out of the school library. A special relationship developed between us and the memories of those times together have remained with me.

Harvey, age 6, visiting the farm of deaf friends. Hilda made most of our clothes. Harvey grew so fast that Hilda and Abe could not always afford to keep him in clothes that fit.

Harvey

Harvey: As summer vacations in Fond du Lac became repetitive and boring, I began to spend more time in Madison at the neighborhood playground on Bowen Court. I fondly remember the kindness and influence of Mr. Schwengle and Mrs. Borman, the playground directors, during those long hot summer days. I bought gimp to make lanyards, learned how to play chess, and played in city marble and chess tournaments. I also played baseball. Being on the roster for the "City Car" taxicab company in the Midget League, and getting my first official jersey and cap was a thrill.

I shined shoes around the Capitol Square for several summers, using a shoeshine box that my dad built for me. I perfected my sales pitch: "How about a shine? Just one thin dime!" and circled the Square, talking with the businessmen and government employees who sat on the benches along the sidewalks as I shined their shoes. On a good day with good tips, I could earn as much as four to five dollars, which impressed my dad. I also began helping with small jobs around the apartments. He praised me and told me that he was proud to see me starting to grow up.

I attended Hebrew school two to three days a week and, although I went, was not overjoyed by it. Many young Jewish children resent having to go to Hebrew school for two hours after spending a full day at school. The teachers were usually University students who worked part-time and who didn't necessarily have good teaching skills. Discipline problems were common; I remember seeing one of my teachers throw a chalkboard eraser at a student, which quickly led to a full-fledged fistfight between the two.

I tried hard to balance the wide range of influences in my life, and often felt as if I were performing a juggling act. While my parents insisted that I behave properly so that they could be proud of me, some of the neighborhood kids had other ideas. My success at Longfellow School "bothered" one bully so much that he sent me a message to show up on the hill at the side of the old Madison General Hospital. There he beat me up "because you got all S's on your report card." I was beaten up another time because our team lost after I was the last one on my team to be eliminated in a game of "Battle Ball." My teammates blamed the loss on me and never quite realized that by reaching that point, I had done better than any of them. The neighborhood gangs operating in the Bush area near our house exerted great pressure on me to become a member and behave as they did. The gang frequently indulged in shoplifting, and I soon found myself stealing from Rennebohm's Drug Store, Schwartz's Pharmacy, and Borsuk's Grocery Store. My heart wasn't in it, though, because I knew I was hurting my family's honor. My dad shrewdly figured out what was going on, accused me of doing the wrong thing, and called me "guilty." By firmly taking things into his own hands, he emphatically cured me of my inability to resist that kind of peer pressure. Several of my fellow gang members later served prison terms.

The Nathensons

After we switched flats with our grandparents, they seemed to manage better for a while, but our mother still had to attend to them every day. Tilly's visual problems became worse, and led eventually to total blindness, caused both from damage to her retina from diabetes and from cataract disease. The local doctors advised her that she would not benefit from surgery, but she would not accept their advice and went to the Mayo Clinic for a second opinion. The doctors there offered her some hope that her condition might improve with surgery, so after prolonged discussions with her family and the doctors, she decided to go ahead. After the operation, her eyes remained covered for ten days. We were present at the moment the patches were removed and witnessed her great disappointment when she discovered that there was only limited improvement.

Meyer, Hilda's father, was also failing; he was unable to care for himself and Abe began bathing and shaving him.

Our dad often carried him the short distance to his shoe repair shop and gently placed him in a chair near the front. Our grandfather enjoyed talking with the customers for several hours each time he was there. In 1949, he fell and broke his hip, requiring surgery which was not successful. He remained very ill following surgery and lingered in the hospital for many months where our parents visited him regularly and Abe continued to shave him. He slowly grew worse, and on July 30, 1949, he passed away.

Hilda's mother remained deeply depressed about her vision and her health deteriorated further. She entered the hospital because of complications from her diabetes and developed kidney failure and chronic anemia. Abe, who had the same blood type as Tilly, went several times to the hospital to donate blood for his mother-in-law's use, but she continued to grow worse. The final months were very unhappy and difficult for our parents as our grandmother became increasingly bitter. On January 24, 1950, six months after her husband died, she followed him.

The death of Hilda's parents was a turning point in the young couple's lives. Hilda's mother had helped them when they had purchased the shop, machinery, and rental property. She also had assisted them in making financial arrangements with the bank. They had come to depend on her guidance and encouragement before she became ill.

In truth, Abe and Hilda experienced mixed emotions at the death of her parents, for although they were saddened to lose the Nathensons, a heavy responsibility was suddenly lifted from their shoulders. Abe was no longer burdened with providing physical support for his in-laws, and for the first time in five years Hilda was relieved from providing constant care. With more time, greater freedom, and a small but important inheritance, they foresaw the possibility of a more comfortable future.

CHAPTER 7

FAMILY LIFE

Our New Home

Until 1950, our family lived in three rooms with Eva sleeping in the living room on a Hide-A-Bed and Harvey in the kitchen on a rollaway that was folded up and stored in a corner each morning. We all shared a single closet in the bedroom. Now our parents were anxious to have a home where the family members would have privacy and a sense of space, which had not been possible during the preceding fifteen years.

During the year that followed we spent many evenings and Sunday afternoons looking for a home. We had no family car, so the realtors drove us from house to house. Abe educated himself with regard to the basic facts of purchasing, owning, and caring for residential property. He began asking questions about heating and utility bills, taxes, bus lines, and other pertinent information. These early experiences and the knowledge we gained by interpreting for our parents helped us later as adults to make informed decisions about buying and selling our own homes.

Our search was confined primarily to the west side of Madison, even though most of Madison's Deaf community lived on the east side where blue collar workers tended to locate. Our parents knew that more professionals lived on the

113

west side and that West High School was geared more toward college preparation than Central High or East High. Another important consideration in favor of the west side was the location of the synagogue. The majority of the Madison Jewish community lived on the west side of town and two new synagogues had been built recently in that area.

After months of searching, we finally chose a house located at 214 North Franklin Avenue on the southwest corner of Chamberlain and Franklin Avenues. It was a solid "older" house, built around 1920, with a sun porch addition, a lannon stone front with large picture windows, and an extra lot (measuring forty by one hundred and twenty feet) forming part of the backyard. This extra lot was a mixed blessing. It required more work to improve and maintain over the years, but it also meant that we had the use of this large space. Years later our parents were able to sell this lot as a separate parcel and realize a good profit.

A consideration which almost prevented our parents from buying this house was that Franklin Avenue had been just outside the city limits until 1948 and was still regarded by some as "the last street in Madison." Chamberlain Avenue, from this corner westward, was an unpaved gravel road. Our house had been the original farmhouse in the area. The second story was shaped like a barn and there was a rural-looking mailbox located at the curb. Some of Abe's deaf friends, whom he felt might have been envious of his success, criticized him for making a poor choice, and ridiculed his move to a "farm." The criticism was painful for Abe, but in spite of this disapproval he had an intuitive sense about the property and felt that he had made a good decision. It is interesting to note that this part of Madison (just five blocks from West High School) is now considered "inner city," reflecting a population growth in the city from 67,000 in 1950 to 191,000 in 1990.

After extensive family discussions, Abe decided to make an offer. All four of us went downtown to sign the necessary papers with great anticipation and elation.

The closing was held on March 23, 1951, at the First National Bank in Madison. We children helped to arrange the terms and financing and interpreted to the best of our ability during the transaction. Mr. Black, the vice president of the bank, was impressed with what we were attempting to do and made us feel important. Admittedly we were nearly as pleased and proud at our performance as we were with the actual purchase of the house. What we did, though, however impressive it appeared to the bank officer, was no more than most hearing children do for their deaf parents. We were transacting business and helping our parents make crucial decisions, which they could have made themselves but for their poor English language skills.

This purchase signified a new era in Abe's life. He was now the proud owner of his own three-bedroom home. Finally both his children would have separate bedrooms. He was proud that we would attend West High School where he was sure that we would receive a good education in preparation for college. The idea that we might not want to go to college was never even discussed.

In addition to purchasing the house, our parents also bought some of the furniture, draperies, and other items that were offered for sale by the previous owners. How excited we were that there would be rugs covering the floors! We would own furniture of a quality that we had never imagined for ourselves. This included a large kitchen table and chairs, a dining room set, two bedroom sets, and most of the living room and sun porch furniture. Games, sports equipment, and other small treasures were "thrown in" with the major purchases, and we were overjoyed to own two pairs of boxing gloves, a punching bag, weights, board games, and even a fake fireplace with logs and a red light to make them glow.

Our move into our new home was relatively easy. Since we were going from three rooms to seven, we did not have much furniture or many personal belongings to move from Regent Street to Franklin Avenue. Most of our furniture was already in the new house.

214 North Franklin Avenue

Abe and Hilda in their new home in 1952 as they begin to enjoy a more comfortable future.

One detail concerning the extra lot had never been discussed. As the offer to purchase had been made toward the end of the winter when snow still covered the ground, our family could not have known that the previous owners, instead of caring for the grass on the extra lot, had attempted to suppress its growth by covering the ground with cinders. Abe was very angry when the snow melted and weeds grew instead of grass. During the years that followed, it would be a constant source of irritation to him that the family had to remove the cinders laboriously by hand and add yards of black dirt and new grass seed.

When Abe and Hilda bought the house, they had enough money for the down payment, but they needed additional funds in cash to pay for the furniture. They tried to borrow from relatives, but their good friend Willard was the only person willing to lend them the cash they needed. He had complete faith in Abe, knowing that he was a hard worker who would repay him. Abe had always been true to his word and Willard respected him. He was not disappointed.

A few years later, Willard also helped Abe build a large outdoor fireplace to serve as a barbecue. It was located in the middle of the extra lot in our backyard where the cinders had been. In the years that followed, that fireplace, built brick by brick by the two friends, provided our family and deaf friends with hours of fun and socialization and many delicious hamburgers. Years after Willard's death, our parents still reminisced about the loan, that warm act of friendship which signified Willard's trust in them.

Work

In addition to attending to the details of the move, Abe still had to operate the shop, which meant greeting customers, repairing shoes, buying leather, and maintaining the machines. Sometimes he was forced to close the shop temporarily in order to show and rent the Regent and Main Street apartments (eight in all) or deal with specific complaints and demands of the tenants. Hilda helped him and so did we, but Abe carried the major responsibility for all of this. He worked in the shop ten to twelve hours a day during the regular workweek and another eight or nine hours on Saturday. In addition, he and Harvey often washed walls or painted an apartment at night.

It was never hard to find Abe. He stood at his machines or at his anvil pounding shoes day after day. The deep grooves worn into the floorboards testify to the many hours that he stood there. If he was not to be found in the shop, he was usually next door attending to one of the apartments or at Kindschi Leather Co., buying leather or picking out a special item for custom work. Of course, while Abe was attending to these duties, the shop had to remain open, so Hilda or one of us would stay in the shop to accept or return shoes. There were no ifs, ands, or buts for us. When he left the shop, someone had to be there. In that way he made sure that his services were always available, and he rarely lost or disappointed a customer.

> Eva: Customers kept returning to my dad's shop, because they enjoyed relating to him and some considered it a challenge to make themselves understood. As I grew up I often helped my father in the shop. Although he did not trust me to fix the shoes or run the heavy machinery, he did like it when I dusted the glass display cases and straightened out the merchandise. The floor was continually littered with old shoe scraps and fine dust from grinding the leather on the finishing machine. He appreciated it when I swept the floor even though it never stayed clean for long.
>
> One day I came to the shop to sweep up and to wait on customers. I usually relayed the customer's questions and comments to my dad and then filled out the shoe ticket. A woman entered, caught my dad's eye, and smiled at him. I started to wait on her, but after several attempts to help her, she turned on her

It was never hard to find Abe. He stood at his anvil pounding shoes day after day; the deep grooves worn into the floorboards testify to the many hours that he stood there.

heel and sharply ordered me to leave her alone. She said she was perfectly capable of expressing herself to my father. I felt deflated, and stepped out of the way so that she could carry on the conversation with him. From that time on I made sure that the customers who wanted to talk to him directly, and there were many, could do so without my getting in the way.

Although Abe's shop was open many hours, his business was no different from other businesses in that his work was cyclical. Often the pace was nearly non-stop, but during the winter months he experienced long periods of quiet and boredom. During these periods he sometimes spent an entire day without a customer and he became deeply discouraged, although he knew that when people wore boots they didn't wear out their shoes as quickly. He would sit on a low chair in the cold and drafty shop, wearing heavy boots himself to protect his feet from the cold floors, as well as long underwear and layers of clothing. There, with idle time on his hands, his responsibilities would weigh heavily on his mind. He tried to read the newspaper or *Reader's Digest*, explaining, "I want to improve my mind." He usually became bored or frustrated, however, because he could not understand the more difficult words and idiomatic expressions. He had more success with *Life* magazine. The pictures helped make the words more visual. At home we brought him "easy" reading materials, so he could learn new words and establish a larger vocabulary. Unfortunately, in those days the subject matter of this material was mostly for children and did not sustain his interest. He did not like to read books that were written for "kids."

At most, he would agree to close his shop for two or three days a year: for the Jewish High Holy Days, for a family celebration, or rarely, for illness. He did not take a vacation for the first nineteen years of his married life. He felt that if he was absent for even a short period of time, he would lose business to his competitor, John's Shoe Repair, located on the next block of Regent Street. In addition, he felt totally

Abe and Hilda at Knott's Berry Farm. In 1954, our family took our first long trip to California together.

responsible for the rental properties and could not imagine that he could be away for any length of time without some major catastrophe occurring that only he could handle. The feeling that he had to be available at all times may have been correct during the early years. However, as we grew older, he became more comfortable with the idea that his children might be able to look after things, and eventually he did begin to delegate some of the responsibilities to us. In 1954 Abe took his first long vacation and the family flew together to California. Our parents traveled again to California in 1956, but this time they went alone, taking their first trip completely on their own.

Money

In spite of the cyclical slow periods, Abe remained enthusiastic about his work and continued to flourish. He was extremely careful with the money that he earned and always taught us the importance of spending wisely. He hated to owe money and preferred to be on a cash basis with everyone. Even though he mortgaged his home and benefited from this concept, he was very uncomfortable with it, fearing that his business "might go down," causing him "to lose everything."

He had lived through the Depression and could relate many examples of people who had become bankrupt; he worried obsessively that this might happen to him. As a result he remained extraordinarily frugal throughout most of his lifetime, and only in his later years did he become more relaxed about spending money for such "luxuries" as personal vacations.

It was quite clear to both of us from an early age that no money was available for allowances; if we wanted money for pleasure or leisure activities, we were expected to earn it by taking a part-time job. The job might be doing some work for Abe in the shop or in the apartments, but that kind of work was usually done to "earn" a new dress or a new suit for a special event. We would earn actual spending money by working for other people, baby-sitting, delivering papers, shoveling snow, mowing lawns or the like. When the definition between pleasure and need was unclear (for example, wanting a new pair of jeans), we often felt guilty asking him. It's not hard to understand his attitude in retrospect, but when we were growing up it was very difficult for us to understand his reasoning. In Harvey's sophomore year in high school he was sixth man on the West High basketball team that was eventually runner-up in the 1956-57 State Basketball Tournament, but he left the team, having to decide between playing second-string basketball and working at an outside job to earn personal spending money. In hindsight, he regrets the decision, but at that time he felt he had no other choice.

In contrast to his views on spending money, Abe paid for educational expenses without causing us to feel any guilt. He felt proud to pay for anything connected with education. As the years passed, he began to regret that he had not done more in other ways. Much later in his life he became extremely generous, lending us money and then forgiving the loans, as well as contributing regularly toward his grandchildren's education.

The vivid image of our father working long hours in

his Quonset hut—too cold in the winter, too hot in the summer, without a bathroom in it for forty years—was always in our minds as we worked hard to educate ourselves.

That image evoked a response that helped form our characters. We sometimes feel that we have cheated our own children by taking away the need to work for certain things that we give to them as a matter of course. Likewise, due to lack of financial need, they have been excluded from qualifying for many scholarships, and the sense of self-worth that goes with such accomplishments.

The New Car

We went about choosing our first family car in much the same way we selected our new home. Usually, in the evenings or on weekends, the four of us would visit an automobile showroom. We would look at cars, ask questions, and try to negotiate the best "deal." Then Abe would ask for time to think about it before he made a decision, and he would use this time to visit other showrooms. We followed this procedure for several months before Abe decided to order a car that would be built to the specifications he wanted. In those days the list of options was not as extensive as it is today. Still there were many choices and we all agonized over every one. We finally settled on a two-tone Chevrolet Deluxe Styleline with four doors, black tires, *and a radio*. Even though our parents would not be able to hear it, they wanted us to enjoy the radio on our family trips to Fond du Lac, Sheboygan, and Milwaukee. We were told the car would arrive in six weeks.

We waited impatiently for six weeks, but no car arrived, and after waiting for three months, our dad was really upset. We called the Chevrolet dealer often and were told that a long list of cars remained on back order; Abe learned that he couldn't depend on the dealer's word. Several months earlier Abe's sister Lillian and her husband Ben had purchased a 1950 Nash Ambassador jointly with Abe's parents, and they wrote that they were excited about the good deal they had negotiated. One Sunday, after months of waiting in vain for our own car, our family went with Lillian and Ben to the Nash showroom in Fond du Lac, and that same day Abe impulsively purchased a large rust and yellow Nash Ambassador. The car looked like an upside-down bathtub; years later it came to be regarded as one of the ugliest cars ever manufactured and sold.

The combination of prolonged waiting, Lillian and Ben's enthusiasm, and the "good deal" led to Abe's impulsive decision. We well remember how thrilled we were as we drove our spacious new car back to Madison. Our dad was impressed with the Hydra-Matic automatic transmission, and proud of the 115-horsepower rating; not used to technical language at home, we children interpreted this literally and imagined 115 horses up front pulling our car forward. For the first time we could travel to Fond du Lac or Milwaukee without taking buses. How often we had taken the Greyhound from Fond du Lac, and then to save money, had walked from the station back to our home with all of our luggage in hand (two miles to Regent Street or four miles to Franklin Avenue). Our excitement blinded us to the fact that the car was ugly, and a gas and oil guzzler, as we would find out later. Our dad was again ridiculed by some of his deaf friends for this purchase, but this time the criticism was probably justified. Only four years later, after several expensive major repairs, Abe traded it in for a 1955 Buick, making the Nash Ambassador the most short-lived of any of the cars he ever owned.

Abe was an excellent driver and his deafness posed no special problems. Deaf drivers, in fact, have better driving records than their hearing counterparts and our dad was no exception. He drove cautiously, always looking both ways, checking his rear and side-view mirrors repeatedly. He had fewer distractions than the average driver, for he could not hear conversations or other sounds that might have diverted his attention; he was proud that in over fifty years of driving he never had an accident and never received a ticket for a moving violation. We do recall that he once received a warning for driving too fast in a school zone, but not an actual ticket.

We did worry that he might fall asleep while driving on the highway at night because of the darkness and complete silence. We watched him very closely, suspecting that he might doze off, but he never did. When he felt sleepy he simply pulled off the road, and we all waited while he took a short nap. In later years one of us drove while he rested.

Harvey: My dad had started driving in the 1930s when the Barash family purchased a used Model-T Ford. In those days it was easy to get a license through the mail; no tests of knowledge or driving skill were given. This method was apparently satisfactory until 1939 when laws were enacted requiring driving tests. Abe originally got his license in this way, and it may explain his apparent laxity about the law when I began to drive.

In retrospect, I find it hard to believe that he let me drive the family car at age fourteen, two years before I could qualify for a temporary driver's license. It all started when I convinced my father to let me steer while he was driving. Then I began to operate the gears, and I finally ended up in the driver's seat. It wasn't long before he let me drive to the store on errands. Next he allowed me to drive to meetings at night, and then he gave me permission to use the car for dates. Once he even allowed me to take the car without a license on a date during a winter snowstorm in ten inches of snow! In terms of modern liability, I can't believe that my father allowed these driving excursions, as the risks were enormous in case of a traffic violation or a serious accident. Someone might have been injured or even killed. I rationalized my use of the car by arguing that I was a very responsible teenager and a good student. My parents agreed, for at age fourteen, I was doing their tax forms and handling their business affairs. They did not think it unreasonable that I should be able to drive the car as well.

Like so many other teenagers, I felt invulnerable when I drove. Looking back, I can see that we were all fortunate that my dad was spared the anguish of having to deal with the consequences of a serious accident.

He did have automobile insurance, as it was required by law, and it was also clear to him that fire and liability insurance was necessary for his house and business. However, he never understood the need for health insurance until I was applying to medical school during my last year in college. If any member of our immediate family had been involved in an accident or become seriously ill while we were growing up, the results could have been economically and emotionally catastrophic. All during those years he seems to have been looked after in some special way.

The Telephone

Because we didn't have a telephone when we needed to communicate or make arrangements with anyone outside the family, we had to do it in person. This took time and was inconvenient, especially before we owned a car, so the introduction of the telephone into our home in the late 1940s changed our lives dramatically. It was hard to believe that there was no longer a need to speak face to face; one could simply pick up the phone, dial some numbers, and suddenly we were talking to someone on the opposite end of the phone line. This "miracle" had occurred in most homes in the United States during the 1930s, but not in our home until 1947. If it seemed miraculous to us hearing children, imagine what it must have seemed like to Abe and Hilda! Although we telephoned our friends sometimes, most of our calls were for

Eva on the phone. Our personal use of the phone conflicted with our parents' need for us to place calls for them. They wanted their calls made now!

"business" — asking for information or making arrangements for our parents.

In order to get the cheapest rate we had a party line, which meant that the line was not private. Three or four unrelated families shared it; if one family was using the line, the others had to wait until it was no longer in use. It was hard to explain to our parents the concepts of "the other party is talking" and "the line is busy." Our parents often would assume that we just didn't want to make the call for them at that particular moment. Simply picking up the phone, listening, and then announcing, "Someone else is talking, so I can't make the call now," made them suspicious. They accused us of being lazy and not wanting to help them. We must admit that occasionally we *did* fib and say that someone was talking, just because we weren't in the mood to make more calls. And, since the telephone line was not private, we sometimes "listened in" for entertainment.

The same problem occurred when the line was busy. Our parents saw us pick up the phone, dial the numbers, wait, and then announce that "the line is busy." A "busy line" was a difficult concept for our parents, as they had never heard a busy signal, nor did they understand what was happening electronically when the signal suddenly began while one of us was standing there with the phone at his or her ear. If we announced instead that there was no answer, they usually accepted this explanation readily, perhaps because they could check up on us later on to see if we were telling the truth.

For the most part we didn't mind helping our parents with phone calls, although sometimes three or four different conversations were required for one arrangement. It made us feel important and needed. Occasionally, though, if we made a mistake, we risked making Abe very upset with us.

Another problem connected with the telephone was that it sometimes brought bad news. One of us would have to receive the news, process it, digest it, privately deal with it emotionally, and then explain it to our parents. For example, if a death occurred in the family, we might modify the information to soften the impact. After we were sure our parents understood the news, we then had to deal with their emotional response. Often we had to make additional phone calls in order to clarify the information or to communicate the news to others. Similar problems occurred with face-to-face interpreting — the phone situation only intensified the difficulties. Occasionally someone from school called, requesting that a meeting take place because of a behavior problem (Harvey talked a lot in school). We found ourselves in the awkward position of having to set up the arrangements for a conference about ourselves and then having to interpret the conference! Quite often we would censor the call completely, so that it never reached our parents; in this way we actually controlled the news that came to them. This carried over to radio news reports or to situations in which we changed the content of the message to suit ourselves or to match our Sign Language abilities.

As we grew into our teens we made more and more personal calls of our own, sometimes lengthy ones. Our personal use of the phone interfered with our parents' need for us to place calls for them and occasionally created tension between us. Abe and Hilda usually wanted their calls made immediately. In their minds this was perfectly reasonable, since they were paying the phone bill and they perceived the phone as a necessity for them, but a luxury for us. Being told to get off the phone was (and is) a common experience for both hearing and deaf children, but immediately after we gave up the phone, we were expected to accommodate our parents and place a call for them. Somehow we lived through those years and when we were older, we came to realize that the benefits we received from handling these responsibilities far outweighed the negative effects.

Television

Technology marched on and in the late 1940s, television became available to the average American family. In 1952, a year after our move to Franklin Avenue, we purchased our first television set. It was a seventeen-inch RCA TV-radio-phonograph console, which remained in the family for more than twenty years.

Although television could miraculously bring events of thousands of miles away into our home, it did not have nearly the impact within our family that the telephone did. We learned about new places, people, and ideas, but the information was general, not nearly as relevant or personally useful to our parents as the specific information brought by the telephone. Then too, until recently when programs became captioned, the information offered on TV had no meaning for Abe and Hilda without someone to explain to them what was being said. They often figured out the plot of a melodrama on their own, but they couldn't understand conversations or anything more subtle unless we interpreted.

Thus, a situation developed in our home which was quite the reverse from that in most families: rather than discouraging us from watching TV, our parents encouraged us to watch with them, so that we could explain what was happening. A subtle subconscious interplay developed in which they might call us into the room where they were watching television and try to interest us in the program.

They hoped that one of us would become involved enough that we might decide to stay and interpret.

It was confusing. On one hand, we were encouraged to be good students, which took a lot of studying; on the other, they wanted us to watch TV with them, taking time from our studies. No matter what our decision, ambivalent guilt feelings tugged at us. We succeeded somewhat in our efforts to avoid the TV, but ended up watching more than we might have otherwise. It would be inaccurate to suggest that we always avoided television programs so that we could study or do more useful things. Some of our aversion was caused by the fact that it was difficult to watch a TV program and interpret at the same time. This required excellent signing skills and considerable concentration, and our Sign was not as developed at that time as it became in later years. It was often less demanding for us to read or study than to watch television with our parents!

As the years passed, our parents became more sensitive to our needs; they learned to select programs in which they could follow the action fairly well and to understand when they should not ask us to interpret. Abe loved to watch sporting events and was able to follow the action without the benefit of a commentator. Since he had participated in sports at Delavan, he knew the rules and didn't need outside help. Gradually we were left to our studies as it became clear to them that this was a more valuable use of our time.

Deaf Friends

Most people have different circles of friends. They have friends and acquaintances in their neighborhoods and at work, and meet others through family connections, religious observances, and shared interests and hobbies. These circles may be separate from one another or they may overlap to varying degrees. Abe and Hilda moved primarily in two circles with very little overlap: the two separate worlds of the hearing and the deaf.

During the first half of their lives they were much more comfortable with the Deaf community; they loved going to the Deaf Club. Communication was easy, so they looked for any excuse to get together with deaf friends and they joyfully planned card parties, picnics, birthday and anniversary celebrations. They also looked forward to deaf conventions, where they could get together with old friends from around the state. Only gradually, as we grew older and brought

'We Don't Want Sympathy'

'Be Sensible About Us,' Deaf Urge at Convention

The Wisconsin Association for the Deaf is holding a four-day convention in Madison. The triennial meeting ends Sunday with a noon picnic. Association members shown here are: seated, from left, Mrs. William Binn, Madison; Mrs. Miles Voss, Columbus; Mrs. Harold Schrank, Portage; and Abraham Barash, Madison, president of the Madison association. Standing, from left, are Harold Schrank, Robert Horgen, Madison, editor of "T Pilot," a publication for the deaf; Robert Pagel, Madison, pres dent of the state association; and William Binn, Thomas Hanso Royal Eklof, Arnold Walsvick and Jack Hathway, all of Madiso (Staff photo by David Sandell)

This picture is from an article published in the Capital Times *on June 20, 1964. Abe (lower right) was President of the Madison Association of the Deaf (M.A.D.) at that time. He was elected President three times over the years, and also served four terms as treasurer. His language limitations prevented him from advancing to state-wide office, which required better English language skills.*

our own friends home, did they begin to enjoy being with hearing people.

Our parents were extremely popular within Madison's Deaf community. Both were attractive with warm and lively personalities, and they made many lifelong friends, some of whom continue to be our mother's friends today. Abe was elected president of the Madison Association of the Deaf three times over the years and he also served four terms as treasurer; Hilda perennially was reappointed program chairman or head of the Sunshine Committee. Due to a lack of formal education and his language limitations, Abe could not advance to statewide offices which required better English language skills. State level leadership involved helping to draft and pass legislation that would benefit the Deaf community, and in later years, it included advocacy work. Also, statewide conventions and other events called for interaction with hearing people who used language above Abe's level. Thus, even though his interpersonal skills were excellent, he was frustrated by his inability to communicate well with more educated people. Even though he came to understand why he could not progress to state level responsibilities, he sometimes became deeply depressed over it; sometimes he surmised suspiciously that people didn't like him and conspired to prevent him from higher achievement.

We attended countless deaf parties and celebrations with our parents. At first we went out of necessity, because we couldn't be left alone; paid baby-sitters were too costly, especially since these parties often lasted until two or three o'clock in the morning. Our parents relished these direct face-to-face meetings, and were apt to linger for hours in the days before the telephone entered their lives.

Later, when we were old enough to take care of ourselves, our parents continued to prod us to go to these parties with them. They were proud of us and we knew it. They wanted their friends to see how we were growing, and they enjoyed telling them about our accomplishments. This desire for others to meet us was no different from that of any hearing parent, but their wish was intensified by the fact that they had limited opportunities to express their success. The children of other deaf parents usually came to these parties for the same reason, so we had another group of friends, separate from our friends at school. Some of these children were deaf like their parents. We found it quite natural to play with both deaf and hearing children, but these friendships did not tend to deepen because of wide age differences. Also, these children were from different parts of town or from farms, so we didn't see them outside of deaf activities, and other than the common factor of having deaf parents, we generally did not share other interests. In later years a national organization called CODA (Children of Deaf Adults) was established and these grown-up children have found that they do indeed share a myriad of similar experiences.

Memories of the sights, sounds, and smells connected with those deaf activities are still vivid in our minds. They were held either in tiny, cramped private homes or large, often uncomfortably cold or hot halls for larger affairs. We remember a lot of smoke, especially from pungent, strong-smelling cigars. Cecil Dryden, a good friend of our parents, was the standout cigar smoker. We went to the Dryden home often; Cecil and Florence, his wife, had two children close in age to us, so we always looked forward to going there. Our parents liked him, because even though he appeared cocky, he was jovial and outgoing, and wasn't afraid to say what was on his mind. His blunt statements sometimes got him into trouble and we once saw him come to blows with another deaf man. Happily, it didn't take the two long to settle their differences.

The room or hall in which these affairs were held was usually uncommonly quiet, considering the number of people present, yet within the quiet, we could hear many strange sounds that one would not expect to hear in a roomful of people: grunts, isolated high-pitched shrieks or screams, loud uninhibited laughter, and peculiar-sounding voices. People often would stamp their feet to attract attention through the vibration of the floor. We were totally comfortable with this cacophony of sound, but if school friends happened to be visiting our home during one of these parties, we sensed their wonder or discomfort at these strangely irregular patterns of sound.

At these gatherings we often talked with each other about personal matters. Occasionally we were surprised to discover in the crowd a hearing spouse or relative who had been signing and whom we mistakenly thought was deaf. This could be embarrassing, depending on what we had been saying, especially if we had been making comments about someone at the party.

Our parents' friends were friendly and effusive and often hugged us warmly. They were all sizes and shapes. A few were trim and in good shape, but most of the women were overweight. Some of the men were good-looking, but we think we can say without bias that Abe was by far the handsomest and we doubt that any of their circle of fifty long-time friends would disagree. Due to the large cleft in his chin he was often described as "a Cary Grant look-alike."

In spite of Abe's lack of education and his failure to achieve a state office in the Wisconsin Association for the Deaf, his warm presence and business acumen gave him a position of leadership within the Deaf community. There were no other self- employed deaf men in the area or, for that matter, in the entire state. Most of the others worked as printers or in service areas doing custodial, maintenance, or cleaning jobs. Some were farmers, usually on family farms. Abe owned his own home, owned and managed rental properties, and was the only deaf person in Madison to have succeeded in establishing his own business. Finally, both of us were immersed in studies and bound for college, which at that time was relatively uncommon in deaf families. All of this was extremely unusual for a deaf man, because as a group deaf people were generally undereducated and underemployed in the 1940s and '50s.

A number of deaf friends who might have been consid-

Abe in a familiar pose. He could often be seen pondering life. Note the fireplace that he built with Willard in the background.

ered on the periphery of society gravitated toward Abe and appeared unannounced at his shop or at our home for advice. We remember in particular a deaf man with emotional difficulties who could not look others directly in the eye. After traveling nearly a hundred miles, he would arrive in Madison on the Greyhound bus and come straight to Abe's shop with a small suitcase. He would place this on a chair next to him in a deliberate manner and then began signing to Abe while looking off in another direction, hunching his face down below his shoulder in an exaggerated way. He came to ask advice, to seek friendship, or just to talk. Most other people, hearing or deaf, shunned him, but our dad always readily welcomed him. Abe often brought him to our home for a meal and sometimes invited him to stay the night (thus the suitcase). At first we were afraid because of his strange behavior, but with time we accepted him just as our father had. Abe worked on his problem of no eye contact and "forced" the visitor to look him in the eye by a combination of pleading, insisting, and physically positioning himself directly in front of this man. Over the years we noticed considerable improvement, but of course we can't know how much resulted directly from our dad's help.

> **Harvey:** Recently, this man came to my office, unannounced, in the same way that he used to come to see my dad. He came for advice about a problem and also to tell me how much my father had done for him and what a good man Abe had been. There were tears in his eyes, and in mine, as he signed these thoughts. As always, he had his suitcase on the chair next to him, but this time as he signed, he looked directly into my eyes.

Another long-time deaf friend developed severe Parkinson's disease, and many of his former friends avoided him. This man knew, however, that he would be welcome at Abe's shop where he would sit for hours and just watch, now that it was difficult for him to sign.

When we were children, our father sometimes took us to the home of Mrs. Hook, a blind and deaf woman, and taught us to communicate with her by fingerspelling our names into her hand letter by letter. Although we were frightened at first, we became more comfortable each time we visited, and we loved to watch her face light up as she recognized and identified us as "Barash's children."

A deaf amputee who was confined to a motorized wheelchair after a severe accident often stopped in at our dad's shop. Even if he was very busy, Abe would take time to talk with him, and often took him to lunch at one of the nearby cafés, always insisting on paying for the meal.

Regularly for years our parents drove a mildly disabled deaf girl to and from the Deaf Club for social functions from which she might have been excluded otherwise. Still another girl, with a severe form of cerebral palsy and uncontrollable movements, always made sure to place herself next to Abe while he was playing cards at Deaf Club parties. She admired him and he befriended her. During the *shivah* period (seven days of mourning) after his death, this girl came to Hilda's home to pay a condolence call to the family. With great difficulty, due to problems with uncontrolled body movements, she signed to us in a slow and determined way how much she missed Abe. As we watched her, we were struck by her ability to communicate so much with her bright shining eyes, a special gift she had in common with Abe.

Children and Friends

Leisure time in our early years centered around our parents and their friends, but as we grew older and made our own friends, we attended fewer and fewer deaf functions. Our parents began to feel that we were not interested in them because they were deaf, but this was not true. They had not studied normal child development and therefore didn't understand the natural separation that must occur during these years.

The effect of this was magnified in our family, because our parents had grown to depend on us as the primary link between them and the hearing world. But gradually they came to realize that we must be allowed more independence and they insisted less strongly that we take part in all their deaf activities. At the same time they began to take a greater interest in what we were doing outside the Deaf community and began to attend some of our school activities, if they did not conflict with Abe's working hours at the shop. They sat through long assemblies, even though they couldn't hear what was being said. There was no such thing as an interpreter in those days. They encouraged us to take violin lessons which were offered free in the Madison Public School system and came to our concerts to watch us perform, even though they were not able to hear a single note. They praised us and told us how good we looked while performing, which made us feel proud.

Eva: They strongly reinforced my practice at home as well. Sometimes my dad put his hand on my violin and smiled as he felt the music through the vibrations of the instrument.

The very early years were harder for me than for Harvey. As the first child, I had had more difficulty developing speech without the advantage of listening to an older sibling. Life remained harder even after our move to Franklin Avenue. My shyness proved to be a severe obstacle as I grew older; I did not go out on many dates during my high school years. When I did, I sometimes felt awkward explaining about our parents' handicap to my date. My parents sensed this, which further compounded the problem. It was not until several years after I had passed through adolescence that I developed more confidence in myself and felt more comfortable in social situations. When I met my future husband, Leo Dicker, in 1956, I did not actually introduce him to my parents until after several dates. Earlier, I had had several experiences with young men who had seemed frightened by my parents' deafness and I decided to avoid the issue completely with Leo.

Harvey, on the other hand, was more outgoing and had a happy social and academic experience at West High where he became involved in athletics, was elected sophomore class president, and president of the Madison Youth Council. Unlike me, he dated a lot and instead of being afraid to reveal our parents' deafness, he sometimes used it as a measure by which to judge his date's worth. If his date responded favorably, this was a positive sign; if not, this was a clue to him that the friendship might not be worth pursuing.

My dad loved to write notes back and forth

with our friends, and when they took time to do this, he responded warmly. He liked teaching them how to fingerspell, and many of them used this method as a basis for communicating with him or between themselves (for example, in class when the teacher wasn't looking). He also had fun teaching the signs for many simple, everyday words, and his "students" reacted enthusiastically. Our home was always open to our friends, and they enjoyed spending time with our parents. As we grew older, Harvey and I wondered at times whether some of our friends came over to visit our parents rather than to see us!

Mixed Feelings

In public settings our parents often captured the attention of others by their gracious manners and handsome appearance. Yet at other times as children, we were embarrassed by the strange or unpleasant sounds they made, of which they weren't aware. We were embarrassed by the inappropriate questions they sometimes asked or the jokes they wanted us to tell that didn't seem funny to us.

Interpreting for them made for more mixed feelings. The pleasure of making things clear to them and the pride of having the skill to do it was counteracted by the burden of being tied to them during every conversation at a party or social gathering. We were unable to engage freely in more interesting or complex discussions because interpreting these discussions would have been impossible due to the nature of the ideas being discussed and the limitations of our interpreting skills.

Over the years we began to realize how much they loved to see us succeed. We responded by participating in activities to which they could respond visually, such as becoming class president or playing on the basketball team. We strove to succeed not only for ourselves, but also to provide pleasure for them. Gradually it became clear to us that in spite of their deafness and early poverty our parents had provided a home and love, and had transmitted their values. Our respect for them grew, and strange as it may seem, we were proud of our parent's deafness. Sometimes, privately, we felt thankful that they were deaf because our unique situation earned us accolades when others heard about our special family. Yet these paradoxical feelings of pride were always tempered by the questions that had haunted us since early childhood. Why were our parents afflicted with this curse? What could they personally have done as young children to deserve this loss of hearing? Why did Abe have to pound shoes for a lifetime in his small shop, burning up with heat in the summer and shivering with freezing cold in the winter? Why wasn't he able to acquire language with more ease, to use his mind and unusual grace toward some more noble purpose?

As adults we see the absurdity of our misplaced pride in their deafness, which was clearly a tragedy for them. We now feel profound deprivation at the loss of English language stimulation during our formative years, and know that we missed childhood stories as well as thoughtful, logical explanations to our questions and problems. Yet we celebrate the intense love, support, and values that they were able to provide in spite of their affliction.

Family Sign Language

Within our family, we knew and used most of the essential concepts in Sign. However, these basic signs (sometimes imperfectly formed) were supplemented by speech and lip reading and by other made-up signs called "home signs." The result was a hodgepodge of signed and spoken words unique to our family, which might be referred to as the Barash dialect.

Harvey: This was extended to the naming of people and things (when we did not know the definite signs) by making up combinations of words and signs to identify them. Thus, Dig Watrous, a friend of mine who was thin, played the viola, and lived up the hill, was known as a combination of the signs: "thin - violin - up the hill." Ted O'Dell, who had red hair, was referred to in sign simply as "red hair." And Kent Johnson, who had knee problems, was called "swollen knee," by reaching down and making the sign "big" around the knee.

Given this background, we were sometimes surprised when we met other deaf people who didn't know our dialect. As those instances occurred more often, we realized that we really didn't know formal Sign Language very well at all.

In those years I was considered the better signer in the family. I retained that position while at the University by frequently going to my dad's shop and having lunch with him, consciously learning a few new words each day. The post of "best signer," however, has been taken over completely by Eva, who became first a teacher of the deaf and who is now responsible for the training of interpreters at the University of Wisconsin in Milwaukee.

Abe and his deaf friends were educated at a time when American Sign Language had not yet been declared a language. For over one hundred years educators had tried to "normalize" the deaf population. Speech skills made deaf people appear more normal, while Signs were associated with feelings of shame, and discouraged. Therefore, using Sign was not sanctioned and given the place of honor it enjoys today.

Fingerspelling English words was much more acceptable, and our father often did this in his everyday communication. He looked upon his ability to form individual letters on his hand as an English language skill and he took pride in using new words whenever possible, even if he misspelled them. We both developed an ability to anticipate the word he was thinking of and would spell it back to him in order to reinforce his choice of words. We became strong spellers because of it and Eva narrowly missed winning the school Spelling Bee several years in a row.

Judaism in a Deaf Family

Even though our parents had not been allowed to be married in the synagogue, they remained firm in their Jewish beliefs. Rather, it would be more accurate to say that they carefully followed the Jewish rituals practiced in the homes of their parents, celebrating most of the holidays and following the dietary laws or *Kashrut,* in their home. It is hard to know exactly what they understood about religion and God, because we could not discuss theology or religious philosophy with them. We think that Abe believed that God exists, and we also know that he questioned God's role in causing his deafness.

Because they kept a kosher home, our parents encouraged us to follow the dietary laws, but keeping the kosher laws outside the home was difficult. Eventually, a compromise evolved in which we followed the dietary laws carefully at home, where we had control over what we prepared, served, and ate. In a restaurant, we usually ate fish or vegetarian dishes, and when invited to a friend's house, if meat was served, we ate it rather than risk hurting the host's feelings. However, we all drew the line at pork products and shellfish. Some of us made exceptions to the tenets outlined above, and although Abe was careful within his own home, he often enjoyed ordering a sizzling sirloin steak at a restaurant. This was a carry-over from the environment in which he grew up at the Wisconsin School for the Deaf in Delavan.

Harvey: Approximately one year after moving to Franklin Avenue, I celebrated my *Bar Mitzvah.* My parents were extremely proud and although it was a

In 1952, Harvey celebrated his Bar Mitzvah. *Abe had never had a* Bar Mitzvah *because Jewish law had prohibited him from assuming religious obligations due to his lack of language.*

Family members came from near and far. This was the first in a series of large family gatherings for life cycle events over which Abe and Hilda would preside.

financial strain for them, they wanted to do as much as they could to make this a memorable time for me. My dad never had a *Bar Mitzvah*, because Jewish law had prohibited him from assuming religious obligations due to his lack of language; my *Bar Mitzvah* was an early example of how he would be able to live vicariously through us.

My mother's sister Rebecca came from New York and her sister Rose and her family came from California. The food and pastries were made at home by friends and family members, and no outside catering was used; meals had to be planned for the entire weekend. My parents invited relatives, deaf friends, my school friends, some of my father's customers, and many from the Jewish community. The *Bar Mitzvah* was held at Beth Israel Center where our parents had been among the founders. I led services, chanted my *Haftorah* portion, delivered a speech, and received gifts and good wishes. This was the first in a series of large family gatherings for life cycle events over which Abe and Hilda would preside. Three years before my *Bar Mitzvah*, Eva had been part of a "group" *Bat Mitzvah*, but the event had not been considered as important because at that time women were not expected to fulfill the same religious obligations as men.

Our celebration of the Sabbath began with a traditional Friday night meal. We children sang the prayers over the candles and the wine, since our parents could not, while my dad signed the English translation. After the *Kiddush*, he welcomed our guests, noted any special occasions, and then signed a beautiful blessing, the warmth of which cannot be conveyed by the printed words:

God bless everyone. We should remember those who are less fortunate than ourselves. We hope for good health, happiness, love, prosperity, and peace in the world and in Israel. Amen.

This was followed by our mother's homemade bread, chicken soup, a meat course, European-style potatoes and vegetables, and one of her favorite desserts. This tradition in our family continues today. As the years have passed our Sabbath table has grown larger, to include friends, children, and grandchildren.

Our family did not attend synagogue regularly, nor did we strictly observe the laws of the Sabbath, which forbid all work, writing, riding, carrying, using electricity, or handling money. However, the traditional Friday evening dinner ritual gave us a special family feeling during our growing years. We always tried to plan our activities with friends later on Friday evenings, so as not to disrupt our Sabbath meal. On Saturdays we both usually worked at various jobs or spent time with our friends. For many years, Abe worked on Saturdays out of his own perceived necessity, and only much later, after Harvey and his family moved back to Madison in 1972, did he decide to close his shop to attend synagogue on Saturday mornings.

Although they were not always consistent in their religious practices, our parents wanted us to date other Jewish teenagers during our high school and college years and they encouraged Jewish friendships. The issue was a difficult one for us, as growing up in Madison was largely an ecumenical experience, although now and then an anti-Semitic incident occurred. We got along well with both Jews and non-Jews, sometimes better with our Christian than our Jewish friends. We observed that our parents were closer to their Christian deaf friends than to hearing Jewish people, because of the ease with which they could communicate. At that time, with few exceptions, other Jews did not reach out to them with special warmth or understanding. We were sensitive to this and felt some resentment, so we found their insistence on Jewish dating unconvincing. Looking back we did follow their wishes to a surprising degree, probably out of respect for them.

CHAPTER 8

SEPARATION

We both worried about the inevitable separation from our parents that would take place when we were older. Unlike the average hearing family, whose concerns are focused on whether the children will be able to manage on their own after leaving the home's protected environment, our situation was reversed. Our parents depended on us to help with their problems, and we worried about what would happen to them after we left home. We decided to take certain steps to help prepare them to manage for themselves.

Early Preparation for Separation

We began by trying once again to upgrade our father's reading level. We gave him easy reading materials to study, and then we worked with him in thirty to sixty minute sessions. Although he tried hard, it was difficult for him, because he was tired after long hours of working in the shop. It became hard for us to give this time regularly, as we had our own schoolwork as well. He did make some progress, but it was difficult to measure. He continued to consult the dictionary frequently and tried to read the newspaper, looking up words he didn't understand.

In December of 1956 our parents took their first vacation without us, flying for the first time as well. Our dad closed his shoe repair shop and left the apartments in Harvey's charge. They flew to California for the wedding reception of their niece, Nancy Rabinovitz. We worried about all the things that might go wrong and armed them with notes to flight attendants which carefully detailed their itinerary and plans for changing planes; we also prepared notes to cover other unforeseen contingencies. The flight and the trip went without incident and proved to all of us that they were able to travel independently without one of us at their sides.

Eva: Upon graduation from West High School, I enrolled at the University of Wisconsin in Madison. As a freshman, I joined Alpha Epsilon Phi, a predominantly Jewish sorority, and although I continued to live at home during my first two years I was often away because of classes and sorority activities. My parents felt my absence, but they were not affected to any great degree, because Harvey was still at home and actively involved in their lives. Their dream for me,

Eva met and later married Leo Dicker from Milwaukee, Wisconsin. Her parents' dream for her was that she would find a good Jewish man, get married, and have a family.

147

like that of most typical Jewish parents, was that I would find a good Jewish man, get married, and have a family. Their concern about a degree or career was secondary. I satisfied their expectations when I met and later married Leo Dicker from Milwaukee. Our courtship lasted for nearly two years.

Leo, of average height, had dark hair, a round face and eyes that twinkled when he smiled. Some time after I met him, I asked him how he felt when he first met my parents. He thought for a while, and then replied that he was afraid as he had never met a deaf person before. He felt sorry for them at first, but as he came to know them better, his feelings changed to respect and admiration. His apprehension stemmed from the fact that he did not know how to communicate with my father. My mom was able to carry on a spoken conversation, and Leo soon became comfortable enough to tease and joke with her, but Abe was to be the challenge for him. Leo learned how to fingerspell quickly and soon looked forward to communicating with my dad while waiting for me to come downstairs before our dates. Leo began to learn about Abe's inner feelings, what he thought about, what he liked and disliked, and what he did not know. Leo loved giving him new information, and spent hours fingerspelling with him. In turn, he learned about the Deaf community from Abe, about his shoe repair business, and about the Jewish life our family lived. He observed that our family functioned more adequately than many hearing people he knew.

Friends and relatives who were concerned about my parents took an interest in the young man I was to marry. Shortly after the engagement, our rabbi, Max A. Lipschitz, came to my father's shop and asked, "Is Leo a good man?" Abe nodded his head and smiled warmly and the rabbi left, knowing that my parents were satisfied with my choice.

Eva's wedding day, December 22, 1957. Here Abe and Hilda are about to give their daughter to Leo Dicker in marriage. During the early years of her marriage, Eva and her parents had difficulty adjusting to the separation.

149

On December 22, 1957, Leo and I were married at Beth Israel Center by Rabbi Lipschitz. Mom and Dad were ecstatic. The wedding was beautiful. Working within a modest budget, my parents tried to satisfy all of my wishes. They were amazed at the cost of wedding dresses, and how much the kosher wedding dinner for two hundred guests would come to, but they agreed to everything they could afford. For the first time my father was willing to go into debt for something other than a piece of property or shoe repair machinery. They loved me and they wanted me to have as nice a wedding as other people gave their daughters. My wedding was clearly a symbol of their love for me.

When we married, Leo had just graduated from the University after completing the R.O.T.C. program, and he had an obligation to enter the United States Air Force immediately. I was only in my senior year, so I had to leave the University without a degree. Leaving home was extremely hard for me. I felt that my parents depended primarily on me for business and emotional support, but at the same time I tried to keep in mind that they were fine before I was born and when I was too young to help. I had been out of the house for two years, but I still was not sure that Harvey would be able to take my place, even though he had been living at home, doing all the things I worried about. Other changes were on the way.

Harvey: The situation would have been very different indeed, had I left home that same year to go away to college, as almost happened. I was about to graduate from high school shortly before Eva and Leo were married in 1957, and many of my friends had applied to good schools around the country. I had mixed feelings about leaving my parents at this time, but I was curious to know if I could be accepted at schools other than the University of Wisconsin. So I submitted applications to a handful of colleges outside of the state, knowing very well that it would be impossible to consider going away unless I received a full scholarship to cover tuition and expenses. I was accepted at Dartmouth and at the University of Michigan in Ann Arbor and learned that I was the first alternate to receive one of five General Motors scholarships covering tuition and all expenses. I was told that it was highly likely that one of the first five would decline the award. During the long wait through the summer we all experienced more than a little anxiety. Could our parents stand to lose both Eva and me at the same time? Would they be able to manage completely on their own? Was it sensible for me to be on my own, far away from home, worrying about whether or not I had made the right decision about leaving? We never had to answer the question of whether we, as a family, were prepared to have both children leave home at the same time. The decision eventually was made for us by the other scholarship recipients. All five students accepted their awards, and I did not advance. Our parents were given a four year reprieve from complete separation from their children.

Perhaps if Eva and I had realized earlier that many deaf couples were getting along by themselves without the help of their children, we would not have worried as much. We might have developed an earlier awareness that separation was as much our problem as it was our parents'.

Roomers

Harvey: During the summer following my graduation I worked as a driver at Camp Indianola, just outside Madison. By the end of the eight week season I had made friends with several of the counselors and kitchen

151

staff. When I learned that two people were looking for housing for the fall, I brought Herb Klukas and Yeong Soo Kim home to meet my parents; soon after, my parents invited them to be student roomers in our home. Suddenly, instead of no one in our home (had I gone away to college), we had three University students living there during the first semester of my freshman year.

Herb Klukas had been an all-conference tackle from Prairie du Sac and was attending the University of Wisconsin on a football scholarship. He was short, stocky, muscular, and always smiling; he got along well with both of my parents from the beginning. He ate anything and everything Mom served him, and she, in turn, was delighted by the way he devoured her cooking and baking. He was amazingly strong and could Indian arm-wrestle on an even par with Abe. At times we all became involved, laughing and feeling each others' muscles, doing push-ups, and standing on our heads, just as we had when we were younger.

Kim was much less outgoing and for a short time had some trouble communicating. But he responded to Abe's warmth and my dad soon learned that Kim, too, was a good arm wrestler. He was the first person from a different culture with whom my parents had interacted closely. He was far more reserved than Herb, but I'm sure he felt welcome in our home.

During my freshman year I joined a fraternity on campus, and there I met Phil Lev, who became an important "member" of the Barash household. Phil was from Chicago, lived in the fraternity house, and was my "pledge father." When Phil first met my parents he remembers being afraid, as he, too, had never met a deaf person. He describes Abe as being "big, strong, and fearsome," but as he came to know him better, he soon learned about my dad's kindness and gentleness. He spent many hours at our home that

152

semester and enjoyed the warm feeling he found there. It didn't take long before he and I worked out an arrangement that would serve us both well.

Phil had an obligation to live in the fraternity house for two years, as did everyone from outside the city; since I was from Madison I had no obligation to live in the fraternity, nor could our family have afforded it. We made an agreement to switch during the second semester of my freshman year. Phil moved in with my parents, but continued to pay the bills for his room at the fraternity house in fulfillment of his obligation, and in turn, I moved into Phil's room at the fraternity. This way, Phil got out of the fraternity house which he no longer enjoyed, and I had a chance to live on campus. This arrangement suited both of us. Phil appreciated the warmth of our home at that point in his life, particularly since he had been adopted as a young child and had recently lost his adoptive mother. My parents became "Mom" and "Pop" to him. He called Abe "Pop," and addressed him with the sign used for "soda pop" (pulling the middle finger of the right hand out from the closed left hand and then striking the palm of the right hand against the side of the closed left fist, making the sound of a pop bottle opening). My parents called him "Sonny boy" and

Roomer Phil Lev standing with Hilda and Freda Barash in 1960. Abe and Hilda called him "Sonny boy." Harvey wondered, "Who is the favorite son?"

taught him many new signs which he learned quickly; during that semester their relationship strengthened, and I began to wonder exactly who was the favorite son! Meanwhile, I experienced a semester on campus and learned enough about fraternity life so that I had decided to deactivate entirely by spring. I had become disillusioned with the fraternity, questioning the values, way of life, and the procedure for selecting new members.

Several other people lived in our home in the years that followed, exposing Abe and Hilda to many different cultures. During the 1958-59 academic year, instead of a student, the head of the school psychologists in Tel Aviv, Israel, became our "roomer" for six months while doing post-doctoral work at the University of Wisconsin. Dr. Malenovsky was a well-educated middle-aged man who had moved from Russia to Palestine before Israel was a state. Abe and Hilda were surprised to see this professor studying at night and struggling with the English language. He also had trouble learning to sign, but finally managed to do some fingerspelling. He, too, was moved by our parents' warm hospitality and considered his stay in our home to have broadened his perspective. My parents promised that one day they would visit him and his family in Israel.

During the 1959-60 academic year, Peter Townsend, a graduate of Harvard University, came to Wisconsin to work toward a Master's degree in Social Work. He was introduced to our family by his fiancée, Nancy Miles, one of my old high school friends. He was as different from Dr. Malenovsky as day is from night. He was fun-loving, musical, and had an artistic flair, and fingerspelling posed no problem for him. In contrast Dr. Malenovsky had been more somber and hard-working. Abe and Hilda observed these differences and signed with great animation about the fascinating "world."

During my final year at the University we did not have a roomer, because Eva was due to return to our home with her new baby daughter, Marcy, for several months while Leo was in Japan with the Air Force. But as I was active in the Memorial Union and the International Club, I continued to bring students and graduate students to meet our parents.

My father rented many of the apartments next to his shop to foreign students studying at the University, and instead of being a landlord, he became their friend. He invited some of them to our home on Franklin Avenue for homecooked meals and they, in turn, invited us to their small apartments for specially prepared Egyptian dishes, Japanese cooking, or hot spicy foods from India. Sometimes our palates burned for days afterwards.

Disappointment

Harvey: For many years my dad encouraged me to study business or law. He had dreams that we might start a new business or that we might "invent" something. Together we would become very wealthy. He thought that his Regent Street property might be developed into large apartment buildings or a private dormitory, but he had no real understanding of investment capital, or the zoning changes and politics that might be involved. He often talked about how we might become partners, and later he had similar ideas of going into business with Eva's husband, Leo.

I made the decision to begin premedical studies at the beginning of my third year in college. At first my dad was disappointed, because he could see that his dreams about business would never be realized. However, as he began to understand my reasons, he slowly resigned himself to my decision.

Then, as I began talking about going away to medical school, the idea of complete separation from both children became another source of sadness for my parents. Once again a condition for going away to medical school would be a full scholarship or I could not afford to leave Madison.

In my senior year, I applied to a number of medical schools in the East. When I was invited to join Phi Beta Kappa, my parents had no idea whatsoever of what this meant; but I hoped that my election during my third year, along with the fact that I had taught an embryology lab as an undergraduate, would strengthen my applications. I was accepted at several medical schools and received offers of full-tuition scholarships to the University of Pennsylvania Medical School and

Abe and Hilda celebrate 25 years of marriage on February 24, 1960. Note their "adopted" son, Phil, in the doorway.

the Albert Einstein College of Medicine. Whether or not to leave my parents would be my own decision this time. After exhaustive discussions with relatives, friends, and teachers, I decided to attend the Albert Einstein College of Medicine in New York City.

Guilt

Eva: When I first left Madison with Leo I had tremendous feelings of guilt and I remember crying continuously during the first four hours of the trip and often thereafter for many months. The separation pains continued for more than a year. Leo and I made several trips home and each departure was again very difficult, so that Leo wondered if I would ever be able to leave home emotionally. I developed medical symptoms that caused me to visit the doctor on the Air Force base frequently; after extensive testing, the doctors concluded that my symptoms were psychosomatic. We were struggling financially and came home when we could, but not often enough for me. We were unable to come for my parents' twenty-fifth anniversary celebration and my medical problems flared up again. Although I know that my parents missed me, they were not aware of the trauma with which I was dealing, and I did not want to tell them because I knew it would be hard for them to understand. Psychosomatic illness is a vague concept and would have been difficult to explain.

Harvey: For me, the decision to leave Madison was certainly much easier at the end of college than it would have been after high school. My parents had become much more worldly; they had experienced students living in their home, and they had learned from their tenants and our friends. My dad was also more stable financially, and if he had needed to contribute something toward my education at a private medical school, it would not have been so great a burden. Friends and family members agreed that a separation would be healthy and that the past four years had been good preparation for them to get along by themselves. Before I left Madison, we placed an ad and found a new roomer; it was agreed that the roomer would make all necessary phone calls for our parents.

Part of my plan for separation was to teach my mom to drive a car. If she learned to drive, she could assist my father by paying bills, doing errands, and going to help at the shop. My dad and I both worked hard helping her learn the necessary information to pass the written test for a temporary license. Then we took her on the road. At first we thought she would never learn, but she improved slowly; the process was arduous. She failed the road test on her first attempt only because she didn't look back over her shoulder or use her side-view mirrors enough. The examiner pointed out how necessary this was for a deaf driver and after we subjected her to additional grueling drills, during which tempers sometimes flared, she finally passed her test one day before I left for medical school.

The day of my departure was sad. I knew that I could have remained in Madison to attend medical school at the University of Wisconsin, but I also felt strongly that I must leave Madison for a time. I vowed to myself that someday I would return to settle in Madison. I knew that our parents were proud of us, but I could not shake the feeling that they thought they were being abandoned and that their lives were finished.

Harvey's graduation from the University in 1961 prior to his departure for medical school. Abe and Hilda were proud of him, but he could not shake the feeling that they thought they were being abandoned.

Abe, wearing Harvey's cap and gown, stands with his parents, Peter and Freda. Eva wrote on the back of the picture: "Dad graduates from the school of hard knocks."

Part III

Later Years

CHAPTER 9

EXPANDING HORIZONS

We needn't have worried. Their lives were not finished. Although our parents were sometimes lonely, most of the time they were surrounded by friends and continued their remarkable personal growth. When they could no longer depend on us, they learned to manage with help from their student roomers or from their neighbors. We started having families and they began taking trips to see us.

Close Friends and Roomers

A few years before Harvey left for medical school, Marianna and John Kuglitsch had moved to Madison from Delavan. This warm, intelligent, deaf couple had two young deaf daughters, Debbie and Patty. They moved to a cozy bungalow on the near west side, not far from Abe and Hilda, and eventually became our parents' best friends. John had been Abe's classmate nearly twenty-five years earlier at the Wisconsin School for the Deaf in Delavan, and they had played football together on the high school team.

John was a printer for Madison Newspapers and was more literate than our dad, although this never proved to be a barrier to their friendship. Printing and the operation of linotype machines was one of the most popular trades taught at Delavan because this job required only minimal interaction with hearing people, making it very suitable for the deaf.

Even after many years Abe still regretted that he had not become a printer; he would have liked the good wages, regular hours, and paid vacations. He was also aware that most deaf printers were more successful with the English language than he, as the typesetting process reinforced their language skills. Abe, of course, had begun to learn English at age fourteen, when he entered Delavan, so he was not able to learn the language quickly enough to be trained as a printer. Periodically when he became depressed with his work in the shop and wished that the other career had been open to him, we would have to remind him of his late start at Delavan. We would also stress how important it was that he could be independent in running his own shop and not have to take orders from anyone.

Ironically, with the advent of computers, the demand for linotype operators dropped dramatically, and many bright, experienced, and literate deaf printers lost their jobs. This happened to many of Abe's friends, including John Kuglitsch.

The Kuglitsch children, both deaf from birth, often came by themselves to spend time with Hilda. As they grew up knowing Sign, they could communicate perfectly with her.

Due to their age and handicap, most were not retrainable and they remained without work. Only then did Abe truly understand the value of having his own business; the "paid vacations" and other benefits of the printing trade were finally put in proper perspective.

Both John and Abe loved football, and they often watched the pro games at one or the other's house on Sunday afternoons. They were great Packer fans, especially during the '60s when Green Bay was invincible under Coach Vince Lombardi. While the men watched TV, Marianna and Hilda talked and laughed together; Marianna was twenty years younger than the other three, but they all got along well. She was highly articulate and had a full-time job as a keypunch operator. The Kuglitsch children often came to the Barash home by themselves, to spend time with Hilda. They loved her cooking, and since they grew up knowing Sign, they could communicate with her perfectly.

The Barashes and Kuglitsches took turns driving one another to deaf picnics, card parties, and other meetings, and in nearly thirty years of friendship, we never observed hard feelings or harsh words between them. After our departures, the Kuglitschs became more important than any other friends or relatives in helping our parents adjust to these changing times.

Abe and Hilda continued to have one student roomer a year after Harvey left home in 1961. These roomers helped to fill the empty house and make necessary business calls as well as calls to us wherever we were living. In the fall of 1963, Harry Row, a graduate student in mathematics, moved in and remained with them for the next three years until he was married in 1966. He loved the quiet, spent much time studying at home, and became attached to Abe and Hilda. He remembers being made to feel very much a part of the family. At around ten o'clock, he usually came downstairs to watch the late evening news with them and he tried to answer their questions. Then Hilda would prepare a snack, often honey cake, which was his favorite. If for some reason Harry didn't come down for the news, she would bring a snack upstairs. Soon Abe and Hilda started inviting him down for meals, and by the end of his stay they expected him to come and eat with them if he was there. He remembers that the rent never increased over the three years, although the original agreement was for the room only, not meals.

Harry often joined Abe on Sunday afternoons to watch pro football games, and he, too, recalls Abe's massive arms as he sat in his undershirt. Like Herb, Phil, and Harvey before him, he engaged in Indian arm-wrestling contests with Abe and compared muscle size with him.

Harry made phone calls to us at our homes if there was a problem or news to be shared. He was a good intermediary, and his technique kept improving. He actually put Hilda on the phone, and she would speak or ask us a question. We would then give a loud, short answer or say "yes" or "no." Harry could hear the answer and conveyed it to her by signing or writing. Sometimes she could hear the "yes" or "no" herself, as her hearing loss is not total. Occasionally Abe would get on the phone and try to speak in his low, guttural voice, and sometimes we were able to decipher what he said although he could never hear our answers.

When Harry began courting his future wife, Jane Shapiro, she was made to feel a part of the family as well and was often invited for meals. This practice continued on a weekly basis even after they were married. Harry's father, who was a minister, performed the wedding ceremony, and Abe and Hilda were witnesses. Harry describes clearly how much warm feeling they brought to his wedding. Harvey, who had been observing the growing relationship between Abe and Harry, again wondered occasionally who was Number One Son.

After Harry married and moved out in 1966, Abe and Hilda decided to try getting along without a roomer. In the last five years they had learned to function fairly well by themselves and they wanted to keep that room available for their growing clan of grandchildren who were beginning to visit Madison more often.

Wendy Gordon, the daughter of State Supreme Court Justice Myron Gordon and his wife Peggy, was another precious friend. She grew up in Madison during the 1960s, and came together with Abe and Hilda through her deafness as well as her Jewish background. They shared many rich experiences over the years. Wendy recently recollected:

> Your father was a role model for me. He was like a second father figure. I could communicate better with him than with my own father. He gave me advice. I could talk to him about things like dating that I did not even tell to my own father. It was really something when I met him. I was very impressed. He was handsome, strong, and warm. Imagine, a deaf Jewish man owning his own business. . . my father was impressed with you, your father's children.
>
> I always felt welcome at your home. I could go there and talk and talk. I learned to sign from the Zolas and your parents. Your father had a special connection with the University students. He had so many customers and so many people who seemed to love him.
>
> I was lost. I didn't know who I was until I met them. They helped me form my Jewish identity. They were a big influence on my life.

Grateful to our parents for their interest in her daughter, Wendy's mother Peggy made herself completely available to Hilda. She took her to many different places and introduced her to swimming at the YWCA. Hilda responded warmly and has continued swimming regularly throughout the ensuing twenty-five years. Peggy was nearly as important as the Kuglitches in helping Hilda get along without her children; as long as our mother was busy, she had less time to feel lonely.

Eva and Leo

Eva: After leaving Madison Leo and I spent the next three years at bases in Texas and Kansas, where Leo served as a navigator in the Strategic Air Command. During that time, I returned to school determined to get my degree. After attending Baylor University in Texas and Washburn University in Topeka, Kansas, I received a B.A. in Psychology from Washburn.

I gave birth to Marcy, Abe's first grandchild, on November 14, 1960, in Topeka, six months before Leo was discharged from the Air Force. When Marcy was six weeks old, I took her to stay with my parents for two months while Leo was on special SAC assignment in Japan. Abe loved Marcy, and he had a wonderful time with her; she would be his only granddaughter and eventually she would give birth to the great-granddaughter named after him.

He could not have known then that Leo and I would receive our master's degrees in Deaf Education

Abe with his first grandchild, Marcy, at six weeks. He could not have known then that Eva and Leo would receive their Master's degrees in Deaf Education from Gallaudet College, nor could he have known that this baby and her future spouse would repeat this cycle a generation later.

from Gallaudet College, nor could he have known that this baby and her future spouse would repeat this cycle a generation later, also receiving their master's degrees in Deaf Education and Counseling from Gallaudet.

Leo was discharged from the Air Force in 1961 and was faced with the need to make a career decision. He decided that he would like to obtain a degree in education with a view toward becoming a principal or working in school administration. To that end he enrolled at Beloit College, fifty miles south of Madison. In exchange for being a dormitory housefellow, he received free tuition and an apartment for our small family. I found a position as an English teacher at South Beloit Junior High School. We made regular trips to Madison and my parents also visited us in Beloit.

For one of his courses Leo was asked to write a term paper on some special area of education. Because of his fondness for Abe, it occurred to him that it might be interesting to write a paper about the educational facilities for the deaf in Wisconsin.

He went to the nearby Wisconsin School for the Deaf in Delavan as part of his research. There he spoke with Kenneth Huff, superintendent of the school, who told him of the great need for teachers and urged him to consider becoming a teacher of the deaf. Leo returned home aglow with the thought that perhaps deaf education might be an interesting area to explore, and I became excited about this idea as well, as it was something that I had dreamed about for years. Our decision to enter the field of deaf education was to affect my parents profoundly for the rest of their lives.

Together we applied to and were accepted by several schools for graduate study. We chose Gallaudet College in Washington, D.C., primarily because at

Eva, Leo, and Harvey demonstrating Sign Language for a Capital Times *newspaper article in 1963. Eva is making the sign for "responsibility," pushing her hands against her shoulders to show the "weight of the world." Leo is portraying the sign for "book" by placing his hands together to illustrate an open book. Harvey makes the sign for "study." His left hand represents a book and his right is grasping the contents.*

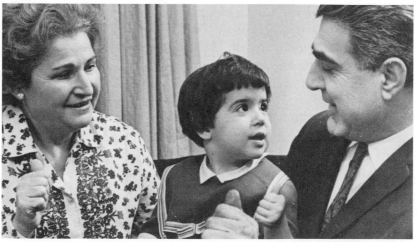

While they beam with delight, Marcy, age three, shows her deaf grandparents she can fingerspell the letter "A."

that time it was the only school that concentrated on both the manual (Sign Language) and oral (lipreading and speech) methods of communication, called "simultaneous communication." Other institutions were heavily biased toward the oral method, but Gallaudet had a special appeal with its simultaneous approach and its many deaf students. There was little support then for the integration of different methods for teaching deaf children, but later the philosophical concept of Total Communication, using a combination of all the communication modalities that might suit an individual child, became well accepted. After our training, Leo and I contributed to this change in attitude within the State of Wisconsin.

At that time, Gallaudet College was the only college in the world offering an undergraduate degree for deaf students. In 1963 Leo and I entered the graduate school, where there were both hearing and deaf students. Robert Horgen, Director of the Wisconsin State Service Bureau for the Deaf and a former Gallaudet College graduate, encouraged us to take advantage of the Deaf community atmosphere there. We were the first married couple with a child to be enrolled in the graduate school and in June of 1964, we both received Master of Science Degrees in Deaf Education.

My parents were extremely proud and drove to Washington, D.C., with their good friends, John and Marianna Kuglitsch, for the ceremony. Ted Kennedy was the keynote speaker, taking the place of President John F. Kennedy, who had been assassinated six months earlier. Our degrees were signed by Lyndon Johnson, President of the United States.

Following our graduation, Leo and I both took jobs as teachers of the deaf in Riverside, California, where we taught from 1964 through 1968; I taught in the elementary school and Leo in the junior high

Leo receiving his M.S. Degree in Deaf Education from Gallaudet College in May of 1964. Note Senator Ted Kennedy in the lower left corner. He was the keynote speaker, taking the place of his brother John F. Kennedy, who had been assassinated six months earlier.

school. We wanted more children but were not successful, so while living in Riverside, we considered adoption. We went forward with this decision and two-month-old Todd was lovingly welcomed into the family. My father in particular showed him great love and devotion, as he had already had experience with two "adopted" sons, Phil Lev and Harry Row.

It was in Riverside that Leo first met Larry Newman, the current past president of the National Association of the Deaf. Larry introduced Leo to the California Deaf community and began to take him as his friend and interpreter to state level meetings concerned with the education of the deaf in California. In 1968, inspired by Larry's ideas for change, Leo enrolled at the University of Kansas at the Medical Center and began to work toward a doctorate in Deaf Education and Audiology. After two additional years of study he received his Doctor of Education degree from the University of Kansas.

Harvey and Trudy

Harvey: While attending medical school in New York City from 1961-65, I experienced a resurgence of interest in Judaism. The Albert Einstein College of Medicine was a graduate school of the Yeshiva University and many members of my class were Jewish. I sometimes went with some of the more religious students to the Friday night dinners held in a small dining room at the Mazur Dormitory. Our family had observed the Friday night customs in our home, but I realized that our own experience lacked the richness in song and understanding that I felt during these dinners.

It was at the time of my renewed interest in Judaism that I met my future wife, Trudy Argand, while folk dancing in Greenwich Village during my third year at Einstein. She had recently graduated from Mills College of Education in New York City and was an actress in a professional group that presented children's plays with Jewish content. She came from a traditional home in New Jersey, not unlike the home that Abe and Hilda had created for us, was my age, and had a brother three years younger, the same age difference as that between Eva and me. Her parents were the same ages as mine and were similarly warm and loving. They invited me for a Sabbath meal and I found a feeling like that in our home, except with more depth and dimension. Trudy and her brother had attended Jewish camps for years, and the family was steeped in music and Jewish tradition. Trudy's father played the mandolin, her brother played the guitar, and the family and their friends often sang together. This part of Argand homelife was far differ-

Trudy Argand, just before her wedding. When Harvey proposed he asked that she agree to live in Madison after he completed his medical studies, explaining to her that he felt he must return there. She understood and has grown to love Madison.

At Harvey and Trudy's wedding. Abe and Hilda were again ecstatic. They had no idea how much Trudy's Jewish values would influence their lives.

ent from what Eva and I had experienced; there had been little music in our home.

I brought Trudy to Madison for Passover to meet my parents and proposed to her during that visit. When I proposed, I asked that she agree to live in Madison after I completed my medical studies, explaining to her that I felt I must return there. She understood, and has grown to love Madison in these twenty-five years.

My parents were thrilled with my choice. They drove to Maplewood, New Jersey, with the Kuglitsch family and met Trudy's parents two days before the wedding. The two sets of parents formed an immediate bond, which grew stronger through the years. En route to New Jersey, Abe, Hilda, and the Kuglitsches had driven first to Washington, D.C., where they had attended Eva and Leo's graduation ceremony.

Trudy gave birth to our eldest son, David, during my final year at Einstein and my parents flew to New York for the Bris. They were ecstatic to have a grandson to carry on the Barash name.

I received my M.D. degree in June of 1965. As I had been strongly advised that I would receive better clinical training in a larger city than I could in Madison, we made our way back to Madison via Chicago where I did my internship. I also completed specialty training in Orthopedic Surgery there from 1966-70. I was then commissioned as a major in the United States Army and fulfilled my two-year service obligation at Fort Campbell, Kentucky, where I performed reconstructive surgery on patients who had been wounded in Vietnam. During my residency in Chicago and army service at Fort Campbell, Trudy gave birth to three more sons, Jonathan, Joshua, and Daniel. Abe was exceedingly proud, as they, too, would carry on the Barash name. Our parents had reason for many trips between Madison and Chicago, Fort Campbell, Riverside, and Kansas City.

Abe's Parents, Freda and Peter

Hilda's parents died in 1949 and 1950, and because of their early deaths they had not been able to see that life would eventually become more secure for Abe and Hilda. In contrast, Peter and Freda lived for another twenty years and received much *nachas* (pleasure) from Abe and his wife.

We noticed, however, that during all those years the basic relationship between our dad and his parents never really changed. Although they were often together for Jewish holidays, anniversaries, birthdays, and other family events, Peter and Freda never succeeded in communicating in any greater depth with Abe than they had when he was a young child in their home. The rudimentary and primitive language they had established at home had been inadequate for anything more than satisfying basic needs. Abe eventually became fluent in Sign, but his parents never learned how to fingerspell; he could also write quite well, but as is typical of many Russian immigrants his parents wrote English in only a crude and imperfect way. Thus, the language basis for a deeper relationship had never strengthened.

We observed that at times Peter or Freda would sit down face to face with our dad and try to talk to him using exaggerated mouth movements. However, the conversations were short and only a few sentences were ever exchanged. At large family gatherings our parents often felt left out, because they couldn't hear the gossip or join in the political discussions. This frustrated Abe and he became resentful and surly; we were young and more interested in playing with our cousins, so there was no one to interpret for them.

Because his sister Lucy was a doctor and was married to a doctor, his mother often boasted about Lucy's accomplishments and her skill in raising five children. Although there was plenty of reason for her pride in Lucy, Abe sometimes declared that his mother "favored" Lucille because she was a doctor. He also suspected that his parents graciously gave her financial help during her many years of schooling,

Abe's mother and father near the end of their lives. They died within a year of each other in Fond du Lac in 1969 and 1970. They left a small inheritance, but the value of their monetary gift paled beside the guidance they had given Abe through his formative years.

which bothered him when he remembered that he had had to borrow money from Willard for the furniture in our new home. Despite these feelings, Abe's relationship with his parents slowly improved through the years, and toward the end of their lives it had become much more civil. He still harbored hard feelings about his early married years, but he began to appreciate their love for him and what they had done for him as a young boy in Russia and America.

His mother and father died within a year of each other in Fond du Lac in 1969 and 1970. Again there was a small inheritance, but the value of the monetary gift paled beside the guidance they had given him through his formative years. Their true legacy to him was the lesson of good, honest, hard work and perseverance.

CHAPTER 10

REUNION

Return to Wisconsin

Eva: When Leo and I decided to return to Milwaukee in 1970, we did so, in part, because I wanted to live within driving distance of my parents. After living there a short while, we decided to build a house; we had saved some money and planned to use it for our down payment.

Our dad came to Milwaukee to see the lot we selected. He liked it very much, especially the old olive tree growing in the front yard, but after looking at the blueprints, he felt that the rooms were too small. When we told him that the scale of the house was limited by the size of the down payment we could afford, he insisted that we borrow money from him in order to build a more suitable house.

Although eventually Leo and I would earn far more than Abe had ever earned, over the years he had managed to save money by working long hours and living a frugal life. His loan helped us to build a more comfortable home; he felt good that he was able to lend us the money and liked thinking of himself as a banker.

Leo had accepted a position as Director of Deaf Education at the University of Wisconsin-Milwaukee. Historically the oral method of teaching the deaf had been heavily emphasized within the Department of Exceptional Education at the University of Wisconsin-Milwaukee, and the Deaf Education faculty that Leo joined when he arrived were all strong supporters of oral education. From his training at Gallaudet and his subsequent teaching experiences, Leo had come to believe that the deaf child should be exposed to English and Sign Language through a variety of modalities. These might include speechreading, speech, fingerspelling, devices to facilitate hearing, and visual aids among other possibilities. Each child could use different combinations of these methods according to his or her needs. This philosophical approach is called Total Communication.

Although Leo had been encouraged to come to Milwaukee and the University because of his philosophical ideas about communicating with and teaching deaf children, his ideas were not popular with most teachers in the local school system and some members of the University faculty. For a period of time it seemed doubtful whether he would be offered tenure, which would surely have meant that we would have to move away from my parents again. However, Leo persisted with his "radical" ideas and continued to expose students to the concepts of Total Communication. In 1976, he finally received tenure.

During the same year it became apparent that the need for interpreters was growing. Under Leo's leadership short-term and year-round Interpreter Training Programs were established which trained scores of interpreters for the deaf who began to work throughout the state. He wrote articles on the training of Sign Language interpreters and published a manual to assist in the training of interpreters, teachers, and students. The legitimacy of Sign Language was evolving step by step.

Leo's concern for deaf people increased in intensity as he participated actively in the formulation of legislation addressing the needs of the Deaf community. He was frequently invited to speak at hearings before the State Legislature. In 1979, during a time of crisis for the organization, he was elected president of the Wisconsin Association of the Deaf (W.A.D.) and became the first hearing person to hold that office. In 1981 he received the Distinguished Service Award for his outstanding contributions to the W.A.D. Although Abe himself had been unable to advance to state-level office in the organization, his wish was being realized through his children.

My influence on the Deaf community was on more of a grassroots level at first. I was hired as a preschool teacher of the deaf in the Shorewood school system and later became a supervising teacher in the Deaf and Hard of Hearing Program in the Milwaukee Public School System. I taught deaf children, supervised teachers, and counseled deaf children and their hearing parents as well as deaf parents and their hearing children. Eventually I became nationally certified and began interpreting in hospitals, in the courts, at legislative hearings, for the theatre, and occasionally for well-known personalities. My most memorable experience was interpreting for Bishop Tutu of South Africa when he spoke at the University of Wisconsin in Madison.

At present I am an Assistant Clinical Professor in the University of Wisconsin-Milwaukee Interpreter Training Program and a part-time Family Support Specialist at the Milwaukee Hearing Society. I have co-authored three children's books about deafness, Sign Language, and interpreting.

Abe knew that he had inspired Leo and me, and he took great pride in our work. We, in turn, told his story. Wherever he went, interpreters, teachers of the deaf, and students of Sign Language wanted to meet this remarkable man. Abe often participated in Sign Language classes in Milwaukee and Madison, enabling the students to interact with a deaf person whose native language was American Sign Language.

Leo's untimely death from a massive heart attack at the age of 49 in March 1984, while he was playing tennis, stunned our family and everyone who knew him. Even though there was a history of heart disease in his family and we knew that he was border-line for several risk factors, I was completely unprepared for the loss of my husband.

His funeral was attended by former students and deaf and hearing friends from throughout the state. The University Faculty Assembly issued a Memorial Resolution which read in part:

He was always active in the community, particularly the Deaf community . . . He tirelessly gave of his time interpreting for the deaf on TV, in synagogues, in the courts, and for deaf individuals and their families who needed his help . . . In the words of his rabbi, "He was indeed a mensch."

Although my father was shocked and saddened by Leo's passing and felt the loss as if Leo had been his own son, he was to be my primary source of consolation during the difficult years in which I had problems coping with the death of my husband. Once again he assumed the role of protector of his "little girl" and showed me great love and kindness. I knew that he wept for me as much as I wept for Leo. He sensed my pain and in his own silent way he comforted me, wrapping his large arms and hands around me and holding me close. In time, with my father's help, I began to recover.

Return to Madison

Harvey: Before moving back to Madison, Trudy and I often looked at houses while visiting our parents on weekends. This started while we were living in Chicago and continued after I entered the army in Kentucky. In 1970, while we were home for Thanksgiving, we saw a beautiful old house in University Heights, which had fourteen rooms and had been on the market for more than six months. Considered by many to be a white elephant because of its age (it was built in 1895) and size, it was in poor repair; the plaster was cracked, water leaks had stained the walls, paint and wallpaper were peeling, sash cords were ripped, the boiler was large and old, and the wiring was inadequate. Yet, except for the problems that would be connected with repairing the home, it was exactly the type of house both of us had wanted for our growing family.

We brought my father to see the house, suspecting that he would consider us "foolish" and advise us to buy a newer home. However, after he went through the house thoroughly, he was enthusiastic and told me to "go ahead, buy it." He had no reservations. He could tell from his experience with old houses that it was a very sound building and he was eager to help me "fix it up," as the problem was more one of veneer than structure. Since he was usually very conservative, his enthusiasm led me to make an offer on the house which was accepted.

At that time, in January of 1971, I had no savings and in fact, was in debt because of expenses connected with my medical education and growing family, so my dad made a down payment loan to me, as well. Although I would soon be earning much more than my father, I would not have been able to purchase the house without his help.

During the years that followed our father made further loans to both Eva and me for home improvements and educational expenses for our children. He insisted on "forgiving" portions of these loans as he grew older, proclaiming that he wanted to do more for us now than he had been able to do when we were younger.

In 1972, my army obligation completed, I returned to Madison to live as I had vowed to myself I

Harvey and Trudy's home in Madison. Abe had had experiences with older houses and told them to "go ahead" and buy this "white elephant." He provided part of the down payment, helped Harvey make repairs, and later loved taking his deaf friends on "walking tours" through its rooms, proudly explaining his role in the restoration. Abe's advice had been sound; the home was later placed on the National Registry of Historic Landmarks and its value has appreciated several fold.

would eleven years earlier, bringing with me my wife and four young sons. After our family had moved into our "new" home, my dad came regularly on weekends for nearly a year and together we solved most of the veneer problems. The more significant heating, insulation, and plumbing problems were corrected slowly over several years. His advice had been sound. Our home is now on the National Registry of Historic Landmarks and its value has appreciated considerably. My dad was always proud of the house and loved taking his deaf friends on "walking tours" through its rooms on all three floors and down into the basement, proudly explaining his role in the restoration.

I had accepted a position as an orthopedic surgeon at the Jackson Clinic and I began to perform surgery at several Madison hospitals, with the main part of my practice carried out at Methodist Hospital.

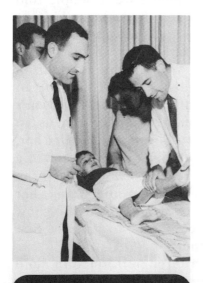

Department of
Orthopaedic Surgery

Upon his return to Madison, Harvey learned both in and out of his medical practice how many people knew and respected Abe. It was not uncommon for Abe's friends and customers to come to Harvey and say: "If you are half the man your father is, then I want you for my doctor."

I also received an appointment in the Department of Surgery at the University of Wisconsin Medical School, where I later became an Associate Clinical Professor of Surgery. My special interests include hip and knee joint replacement and surgery of the hand.

Abe felt proud to have our family back in Madison, and he never hesitated to tell his customers about us; if they had orthopedic problems he encouraged them to come and see me. When someone came to his shop and said, "Your son fixed my hip," he would beam. Similarly, I remember that as I was starting out it was not unusual for a patient to say to me, "If you are half as good at what you do as your father is at shoe repairing, then I want you to do my operation." Or, "If you are half the man your father is, then I want you for my doctor." It was enlightening for me to learn both in and out of my medical practice how many people knew and respected my dad; wherever I went people told me (and still tell me) how much they admired him.

My wife Trudy had been a kindergarten teacher before and during the boys' early years, and was interested in the theatre as well. After moving to Madison she took graduate courses in dance at the University of Wisconsin, and became involved with the Children's Theatre of Madison as a choreographer and as an actress. As my dad's customers began to recognize her, they told him about meeting her or seeing her in a play. When she played the role of Mrs. Frank in the CTM production of The Diary of Anne Frank, her picture appeared in a feature article about the show and he proudly accepted copies of the article that customers brought to his shop.

As Trudy and the children performed in more plays and musicals, my parents began attending regularly. I sat at their side and interpreted for them. It was difficult for both of them to see me in the dark as they tried to watch the stage at the same time. The director,

Nancy Thurow, suggested that I interpret the show standing in a well-lighted spot next to the stage. This proved to be so satisfactory that my parents began bringing some of their deaf friends. Eventually the group grew in size and began to look forward eagerly to each theatre season of four signed plays. As many as thirty deaf friends attended each signed performance. Trudy brought theatre, music, and dance into the lives of these deaf people, and Abe was pleased to know that he had been partly responsible.

Shoe Shop and Work

When Abe first started his shoe repair business in 1935, he had rented a small shop near the University located at 1107 1/2 Regent Street. In 1940 he purchased this building together with a second, larger building located next door. He enlarged his shoe shop in 1945 so that it equaled the size of the other building, but it remained inferior since it did not have running water or a bathroom.

The better building was rented out as a barber shop for twenty years and then as a vacuum repair shop for the next fifteen years. The tenant always had a bathroom, but Abe had none. From 1937 to 1951 when we lived next door, he could close the shop for a few minutes and come home if he had to use the bathroom, but after we moved to Franklin Avenue from 1951-58, he had to make other arrangements, and after the barber shop closed in 1957, we encouraged our father to move next door and take advantage of the plumbing and the bathroom. He refused, worried that he would not be able to rent the vacated shoe shop without a bathroom. He insisted on the inconvenience instead of taking a chance that he might not rent it.

He may have been right, because even with a bathroom it was hard to find a renter for the "better" building; it was vacant for six months and was finally leased as a vacuum cleaner repair shop for $35 a month. During the next ten years he increased the rent in increments to $50 a month. At our insistence, he agreed to write into the lease that he would have "bathroom privileges" and during the first few months he took advantage of this. But in time he stopped because he didn't feel comfortable; instead he went across the street to Wally Schaub's Mobil service station.

In 1971 a situation occurred which was to torment Abe for months. The city of Madison undertook a large road reconstruction project on Regent Street which involved widening the street and installing new sewage pipes; the implications for our dad's business were disastrous. Regent Street was closed for the entire summer and there was no access to his shop, except by parking several blocks away and then making one's way through the dirt and grime of the torn-up street. Our dad was infuriated by the loss of business and the time he spent idle bred more discontent. He wrote us long letters (we wish we could find them), complaining bitterly about this injustice, and we sensed great sadness in addition to his anger.

Although he was not the only small businessman to suffer this inconvenience on Regent Street and many were up in arms about the situation, the *Capital Times*, in an article on May 26, 1971, featured Abe on the front page explaining what the road reconstruction had done to the small businesses on the street.

In spite of his better judgment our father became somewhat paranoid during difficult times, suspecting that others were "against" him. He focused on his competitors, resenting the competition down the street from John, and later from Salvadore Franco, who took over the shop from John in 1979. He harbored suspicions that the other shoe repairmen in Madison were learning new and modern shoe repairing techniques and were conspiring against him, not sharing their secrets because he was deaf.

Such feelings had become less frequent by this period of his life, but the Regent Street reconstruction project caused him to have a temporary setback. He told us that he had

Four Months, No Customers

Regent St. Closing Disaster to Shops

By DAVE MARANISS
(Of The Capital Times Staff)

From the medical complex on the corner with Park Street to the vista of thick green elm trees just beyond the triangular intersection with Breese Terrace and Little Street, Regent Street is dotted with low-lying brick buildings and q u o n s e t huts.

On an average weekday about 20,000 cars are rushed up and down the convenient route between Madison's West Side and downtown, past the small shops which offer such services as photo finishing, vacuum repair, organ lessons, and shoe repair, and such goods as food, gas, furniture, liquor, books, bratwarst and beer.

No one will be rushing down the thoroughfare this summer. The City of Madison and Dane County have begun a joint project to reconstruct Regent Street — at a cost of about $270,000 — from the 900 to the 1500 blocks.

In a rare, but — according to the City Engineering Department — necessary, procedure, the street was closed completely on May 10, and will not be opened for traffic until early September. "If we can possibly keep a street open, we do it," one c i t y engineer explained. "But there were just too many factors i n v o l v e d in this project."

The Madison Crushing and Excavating Co. has been con-
(Continued on Page 4, Col. 7)

Caterpillars, cranes, dump-trucks and chunks of cement have replaced cars and pedestrians on a six block stretch of Regent Street which has been closed for the summer months for a "civic improvement" project.

The Capital Times, *in an article May 26, 1971, featured Abe on its front page, explaining what the road construction had done to the small businesses on Regent Street. Abe was infuriated by the loss of business and wrote us long letters complaining bitterly about the injustice.*

Abraham Barash stands in front of his small, lively shoe repair shop on Regent Street. His b u s i n e s s has been severely affected by the construction project which has isolated the area. (Staff photos by Bruce M. Fritz)

189

visited the modern shoe repair shop of a competitor in the University area; his competitor had shown him around, pointing out and mentioning the cost of each new machine, and then had "made me feel low" by demonstrating how each pair of repaired shoes was wrapped separately in a new brown bag and stapled with the ticket on the outside. He saw that this braggart was flourishing at the very time he was forced to be idle. He replied, inappropriately but proudly, that although this competitor was succeeding in his business, he could not claim three "doctors" (doctoral degrees held by Lucille, Harvey, and Leo) and other advanced degrees in his family, as Abe could! Abe managed to survive that summer, but not without severe stress, and Hilda remembers how difficult it was to comfort him.

> **Harvey:** Three years after I returned to Madison I persuaded my dad to enlarge his shop by connecting the two buildings, so that he would finally have access to his own bathroom. He resisted at first and was hesitant to put major capital into the building, as he felt that there would probably never be another owner. We studied the possibility of building a new shop on the same site, but it would have been complicated and costly. Also, he would have been required to close his business during construction, and another period of time without work would have been difficult for him psychologically.
>
> After exploring the options he agreed to the enlargement and gave notice to the vacuum repairman to vacate. My dad insisted that he and I do as much of the work as possible ourselves; only the electrical work and the actual construction of the connecting passage between the two buildings were subcontracted. We did the rest, including installation of a new floor, ceiling, insulation, and paneling. He was content because he was able to remain open while the work progressed, only closing the shop for two days while

The shoe shop (right) at 1107 1/2 Regent Street, circa 1940. The shop had no bathroom and was poorly insulated. Note Sam's Barber Shop on the left.

Abe's enlarged shoe shop after the two buildings had been connected. The shop was closed for only two days during the three months of remodeling. Most of the work was done at night or on weekends.

the connecting passageway between the buildings was created. A blowtorch was used to cut out the adjacent sections of the metal walls, after which the passageway was constructed. We did our work at night or on weekends during the spring and summer of 1975 and finished the project in just over three months.

The new part of the shop, where the bathroom was located became the main entrance and counter area; the old section, where he would continue to do his work, housed the machinery. The front door and windows of the old section were covered by a large new sign, and mirrors were positioned so that no matter where Abe was, he would be able to see if someone had entered the shop.

In fifty-two years there had never been a robbery or burglary attempt in his shop. One of his customers surmised that this was because "he had the respect of the people. . . he did good, honest work." We advised him not to resist or fight back, should there ever be an incident, because a thief might do something unpredictable and irreversible. He found this unnatural, but agreed.

With the added room and wall space in the new part of the shop, he decided to hang family pictures, letters from customers, and stories written by his grandchildren; he also hung copies of the articles written about him in the state and local newspapers. His customers enjoyed discussing this interesting "gallery" while visiting with him via notes.

Abe's business had grown steadily and after enlarging the shop he became even busier. Instead of worrying about slow periods he began to worry about what he would do when he became sixty-five if he remained as busy. Who would help him? Should he have a helper now? Should he think about selling the business and working for a new owner? We discussed the problem without coming to a solution. He had had temporary deaf helpers through the years but never on a permanent basis, since the business was cyclical and could

Customers enjoyed discussing Abe's "gallery" while visiting with him via notes.

not support two people. If a helper was working and business was slow Abe would become restless and the helper uncomfortable in the tiny shop with no work to do.

On a few occasions Abe had agreed to accept students from vocational rehabilitation programs or from other training situations, but each time Abe had had problems communicating with these students. Often they were inexperienced, and Abe worried about slowing down and falling behind in his work.

In 1976 he agreed to hire a pleasant and intelligent hearing man, Ron Warshansky, who already had some experience. The plan was to train him so that when Abe retired, Ron would be able to take over the shop and either purchase it or rent it; perhaps Abe then would work for him part-time. The arrangement worked well for a while, and there was some advantage to having a hearing person at the counter, but as the months passed problems arose. Ron had dependents to support and needed a steady salary; he wanted regular increases as he improved.

Many customers preferred to talk to Abe directly, so they would be sure to get exactly what they wanted, and business aside, they enjoyed talking with Abe. The thirty-year-old machines, running for longer time periods since there were two men working now, broke down more frequently and repairs had to be made. As the repairman for the Landis stitcher traveled from state to state, he often was not available for two or three days. The lost time was costly and aggravating for Abe. The breakdown of his machinery coupled with Ron's requests for raises made our father uneasy, so after trying for nearly a year to make this plan succeed both Abe and Ron agreed to discontinue the arrangement. We all learned from this trial, Abe's longest attempt at being an employer, that it was unlikely he would ever successfully employ someone to work for him or be able to turn over the management of his shop to anyone else.

In 1978 when he became sixty-five, we felt that rather than consider retirement, he should continue to work in the shop with shorter working hours. We celebrated his "retirement" by posting a sign on the front of his shop announcing the shorter hours. The old shop hours had been from eight in the morning to half past five and the new ones were from ten to three, reducing the official hours from nine and one-half to five hours a day. As he was to start receiving Social Security benefits, he could no longer legally earn as much money without returning a significant amount of it in taxes, so we prepared another sign for him to point at, which read, "Sorry, I am now on Social Security and must accept less work."

The signs seemed to help him deal with pressure from his customers and the large work volume, but we were suddenly faced with a problem we had not anticipated. Our father became deeply depressed. He had tried for many years to develop hobbies and other interests, but had never devoted the necessary time to them because of his need to work long hours. His work ethic was so strong that he did not understand the value of leisure time, and his language ability remained limited as well. The reduced hours that we had imposed on him caused him to become melancholy. His work was his identity and he felt his self-worth slowly being stripped from him.

NOTICE

Sorry, I am now on Social Security and must accept less work

Thank You

We celebrated Abe's "retirement" by posting a sign on the front of his shop announcing shorter hours. As he hated to refuse customers, this sign was prepared to help him explain why he had to turn work away.

During that time, he had a series of medical problems that further undermined his self-image, as good health was necessary for him to succeed in the shop. He had had some dental work done and while on pain medicine he fainted in synagogue during the High Holy Days. Later he had a short period of double vision that was thought to be due to a temporary reduction of blood flow to the brain, and on another occasion he developed a rapid heart rate and abnormal rhythm that was corrected with medication. These medical problems lowered his self-esteem and further fed his depression.

He kept working, but without his broad smile and normal enthusiasm, and he talked about quitting work and selling his shop. We tried to make him understand that selling the shop would only give him more time with nothing to do. It was hard to reason with him, and we weren't sure what we should do. His sister, a child psychiatrist, suggested psychiatric consultation, but we were afraid that he would misinterpret the intent. His friends, John and Marianna, could see what was happening, but were not able to help.

Harvey: About six months earlier I had started jogging and I began to encourage my dad to come with me. At first he said it was a foolish idea, but we cajoled him and eventually he agreed to go. It was mid-winter when I first took him to the University Shell where I had been running regularly for six months. He started by running the equivalent of a block after which I checked his pulse; he repeated this pattern several times and gradually increased his distance while I checked his pulse less often. Within a few weeks he was able to run a mile at a time without problems, and after several months he was running three to four miles.

The family bought him new jogging shoes and a membership to the University Shell for his 65th birthday. He added calisthenics to his routine and

The varied faces of Abe as he "talked" with his friends and customers in the shop. They enjoyed communicating by writing notes, gesturing, signing, and lipreading.

Abe at work operating the powerful "Landis," trimming shoes by hand, and making change.

extended his distance to five or six miles, as we continued to jog together regularly on my afternoon off and on weekends. Many of his customers, who were also "regulars" there, encouraged him and gave him the "thumbs up" sign, to which he responded by beaming broadly. He was becoming a familiar sight at the Shell.

After six months of feeling low and depressed, he admitted that he felt strong and was encouraged by his endurance. He returned to his work with renewed vigor. Not long after, we noticed that he had covered over the "ten to three" sign with white tape and still later that he had penciled in new hours of nine to five. He had arrived at this compromise on his own. His "retirement" consisted of a reduction in hours from his usual extended day, six days a week, to the normal eight-hour day, five days a week. Later he told us that "jogging saved my life."

A few years later in 1981, further improvements in his shoe shop were paid for by sheer "good fortune." Someone lost control of a car while turning into a driveway near the shop and smashed through the front window, luckily injuring no one. As a result the entire front of the shop was replaced, courtesy of the driver's insurance company.

Electronic Devices

Harvey: After I returned to Madison, my dad often came to our door unannounced with an urgent request. He might ask me to place a call to Eva and Leo in Milwaukee, to make a dentist appointment, or to give him advice about some correspondence. Most of the time there was no true urgency. These requests were the type that hearing people handle by making a few phone calls. As much as I loved my dad I sometimes found it annoying to be forced to drop whatever I was doing, to socialize (perhaps offering coffee and des-

Abe looks disbelievingly at the new Toyota that smashed through the front window of his shop. The driver had lost control of his car on the rain-slick street. A newspaper photographer driving by snapped this photo for the Capital Times.

sert), and then to carry out the request. But it was hard to refuse, given our basic relationship and all that my dad had done for me.

When the TTY (Teletype), later called a TDD (Telecommunication Device for the Deaf), was introduced into deaf homes it was a great boon for our parents as well as for us. The original units were large teletype machines which had been discarded and then donated to the Deaf community by Western Union. These machines had been used to send telegrams and were being replaced by more advanced equipment, so they were now made available at a low cost.

They looked like large old-fashioned typewriters and worked by producing a different signal for each key on the typewriter. The user placed the telephone receiver into a "coupler" which connected the phone to the teletypewriter and the signals were then transferred via coupler through the phone lines. A person at the other end of the line with a similar instrument could receive these signals through a coupler, and the keys on the receiving device then would type out the message. The technology had been worked out years earlier, but was never practical for the deaf because the original units had been too expensive.

When these teletype machines became available for private home use by deaf people it was as revolutionary as the introduction of the telephone into our home in the 1940s. Now we could call our parents or they could call us and we could have a direct "phone conversation." The urgent requests could be handled by phone and special trips back and forth between Abe's and Harvey's houses weren't as necessary any longer.

We obtained our first TTYs in 1975, and Eva remembers the New Year's Eve conversation from Milwaukee when she and Leo talked directly to our parents for the first time. Thereafter, the technology advanced rapidly. The TTYs were replaced eventually by smaller and more compact electronic units called TDDs, which were portable and less expensive, so they were made available in more places. Thus, our parents became even more independent; they could call friends who had TDDs and even tried to make some business calls themselves. Often they weren't successful, but they had made a start. Legislation was passed to reduce the long distance rates for TDD users, since the "conversations" took much longer to execute. Our parents now could call Milwaukee directly, and often did so.

More recently the Message Relay Service was introduced in many states throughout the country and in Madison on a part-time basis. This service provides a connection between the deaf TDD user and the hearing person or business that has no TDD. The Message Relay Service receives the input by TDD and then communicates it orally to the other party on a second line. Likewise, the reverse can be done. A hearing person or business can call the Message Relay Service by regular phone and ask the service to communicate by TDD with a hearing-impaired party. These advances and services enabled our parents to make telephone calls themselves after many years of having to depend on us. The limitations imposed by language level and typing ability still existed, but the breakthrough was dramatic. Our mother assumed most of the telephone duties, because her typing skills were better; nevertheless, together they became more self-reliant, making more and more arrangements by themselves.

> Harvey: After my dad experienced his rapid heart rate problem, we recognized that he needed to be able to communicate with us or the hospital in an emergency. A phone was installed in his shop and I worked out an emergency message using a regular phone and a tape recorder. My dad could then send a prerecorded message after dialing the operator on his phone; we practiced the mechanics every week, but the system was not flawless and I never felt completely confident that it would be reliable. Today TDDs have advanced

When the TTY was introduced into deaf homes it was a great boon for our parents as well as for us. The original units looked like old fashioned typewriters. They worked by transmitting different signals by phone through a coupler.

The TTYs were replaced by smaller and more compact electronic units called TDDs, which are portable and less expensive.

to a state wherein a prerecorded emergency message can be sent via the phone jack by simply pushing the "send" button on the unit.

Even though in later years we had both become better signers, we still did not enjoy watching television with our parents, for it required a concerted effort to explain what was happening. So, when "decoders" became available to the deaf in about 1980, we were thrilled. The decoder, which can be used with an ordinary TV set, is another electronic device which has opened a world of new information to deaf people. This device captures television signals and produces simultaneously printed captions on the television screen, enabling a deaf person to read what the person on the screen is saying. Again, there is the limitation that the viewer must be able to see, read, and understand English adequately.

Programs carrying the necessary signals are referred to as "closed-captioned" and are designated by this special symbol in the TV schedules: [☐]. At first there were only a few closed-captioned programs; however, cable television has made many more programs and movies available. Recently Channel Three in Madison introduced early and late evening news reports with closed captions. Today many newer movies on videotape are made with closed captions, so that the VCR continues to add to the amount of understandable programming. Recently, legislation was passed which requires that all TV sets sold in the United States have built-in decoder chips. The insertion of this inexpensive chip soon will enable a deaf person to access captioning on any set.

Our parents were thrilled and grateful for these advances in technology, which enabled them to watch programs by themselves for hours, and to understand most of what they saw.

Harvey: One day I was surprised and amazed when my parents called me by TDD and asked, "Did you see the ten o'clock news? There was a very interesting report about . . ." That call and others like it reflected the important role that electronic devices had come to play in their lives.

CHAPTER 11

GOLDEN YEARS

Judaism Revisited

Historically Jewish Law put deaf people in the same category as minors and imbeciles, because these groups shared the inability to understand the spoken and written word. It was thought that since deaf people could neither hear nor speak, they could not possess the language necessary for participation in religious or secular life. Because they could not say the blessings, they could not be counted as part of a public Jewish service; lacking language, they were also thought to lack understanding, so they were exempted from civil and criminal laws.

Jewish Law changes as circumstances alter, and since it is now acknowledged that the Deaf have language, Jewish Law has been reinterpreted to extend religious and legal rights to deaf people.

Some fifty years ago when Hilda and Abe were married, the question had not been completely settled. The young couple was married in the more secular Workman's Circle Building, not in the synagogue; we have been told, although we can not establish this as fact, that they were not allowed to be married in the synagogue. Whether or not that is correct, it is a fact that for many years Abe and Hilda were

207

not a part of the religious life of the community. They sat in the back of the synagogue hour after hour in silence without understanding the High Holy Day services. They went to weddings and funerals without knowing what was being said; we wonder how much they understood of their own wedding or of Harvey's Bris or Bar Mitzvah. Ironically, they would occasionally attend a church celebration at which a minister conducted signed services.

It was Trudy and her parents who helped to add richness to Abe's Jewish life. Her parents, Annabelle and Leo Argand, had always been strongly committed to Judaism and in 1970, they decided to move to Jerusalem. Early in their marriage Trudy and Harvey attended synagogue, taking the children with them when they were old enough. They tried to create a festive feeling around the Jewish holidays throughout the year, and Sabbath dinners were a highlight of each week as the families congregated at one or another of the Barash homes.

This family activity kindled in Abe a new interest in Judaism, and he began to close his shop on Saturday morning to attend services. At synagogue he saw his children and grandchildren participate in the religious services. Members of the congregation began taking an interest in him and several people learned how to fingerspell. They carried on conversations with him, and tried to help him understand the rituals. Sometimes Cantor Prombaum even signed to Abe from the pulpit. Harvey interpreted the sermons, and Abe followed his hands and eyes intently; if the sermon was boring or repetitive Abe sensed this, could not pretend otherwise, and his eyes would slowly close.

Rabbi Feinberg firmly believed that a deaf person should receive the same honors as a hearing person. It was thrilling to watch Abe as he was called to the Torah for the first time in his life to recite the blessings; he signed the English translation, since he could not read Hebrew, but all those present felt that he had been understood. Later Abe received many more such honors. He even was called to the

Torah to recite the blessings on the High Holy Days, a most special honor. After Abe finished signing, Mr. Rothblatt, the Torah Reader, an older scholar in the congregation who had taught himself to sign, fingerspelled "A-M-E-N."

Over the years Abe came to be highly respected in the synagogue and he radiated spirituality and grace. He had progressed from not being allowed to be married in the synagogue to being fully accepted, and finally, to being honored and even revered.

Travel and Recreation

Eva: After their first plane trip in 1956, our parents did not fly alone again until 1964 when they went to New York for David's Bris. In 1965 they flew east for Harvey's graduation from medical school. They became even more seasoned travelers each time they visited Leo and me in California during the late 1960s. In the early 1970s they began attending the annual conventions of the National Congress for the Jewish Deaf in New York, Chicago, Cleveland, and Los Angeles. As Leo and I were not living in the same city with our parents, we accompanied them to these conventions as often as possible in order to spend more time with them.

Our parents left the United States for the first time in 1977 when they traveled with Leo and me to Israel. Although they had interacted with foreigners in their hometown, experiencing another country's culture and terrain was an awakening for them. Several years after Leo's death I led interpreted tours for the deaf to Greece and then to China; my parents came along, as they said, to keep me company and to learn more about the world. These trips, to Greece in 1985 and to China in 1986, were highlights in their lives and again exposed them to vastly different cultures.

In China they saw firsthand a society of one billion people and became more aware of the problems in that area of the world. Abe became newly mindful of the concept of American freedom. He would never have thought of a visit to China in earlier years. How could he have imagined himself standing at the Great Wall or dancing with Chinese school children?

Abe's friend John Kuglitsch was an avid sports fan and fisherman. His language skills enabled him to read and understand the sports page and other material, so he took a great interest in sports at all levels. He often invited my dad to join him at sporting events, and sometimes Abe accepted, although he usually refused because he was too busy working. John also asked my dad to go fishing with him, but recalls that he accepted only once.

Another facet of Eva's work for the deaf was leading interpreted tours to Greece and China. Abe and Hilda went along "to keep her company and to learn more about the world."

Abe in China in 1986, dancing with children in a kindergarten classroom. There he learned to appreciate anew the concept of American freedom. The thought of a visit to China would never have occurred to him in earlier years.

In 1982 Leo bought a sixteen-foot fishing boat and invited Abe to go fishing with him on Lake Michigan. Although Abe went along reluctantly at first, each trip whetted his appetite, and he began to accompany Leo more often. Sometimes he and Leo spent an entire day fishing, and Abe began to experience the thrill of a successful catch. Later his good friend John Kuglitsch joined them on these excursions. Abe often proudly called attention to a picture of himself hanging prominently in his "gallery" which showed him holding a large fish. I think that on these fishing trips he came as close as he ever could to truly enjoying himself away from his work.

Harvey: After he began running in 1978, my dad became an avid jogger and continued to jog until one or two months before he died. We used to go to the

University Shell every Wednesday afternoon and on weekends for over a year, until I was forced to stop running inside because of an allergic reaction to something in the Shell. Then we began to run outdoors. Some of the friends my dad had made at the Shell wondered what had happened to him and came to his shop to find out if he was all right.

When I was unavailable or had to work late at the hospital my dad began to run by himself. We didn't think that it was safe for him to run outside during the winter months, so he had the idea of running in his basement. He created a route from one end of the basement into a second basement room and back, and figured out that one hundred of these laps

Abe with his friend John Kuglitsch. While fishing Abe came as close as would ever be possible to truly enjoying himself while away from his work. He loved experiencing the thrill of a successful catch.

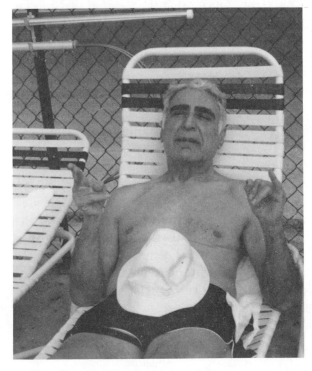

Abe "clowning around" with Harvey and Trudy (above) and spelling "hi" with two hands while relaxing (left).

made approximately one mile. Often he would proudly announce that he had run four or five miles that morning. I found it unbelievable that he could run five hundred laps repeatedly without becoming bored, and I jokingly suggested that he take a loop around the furnace for a change in scenery!

My dad loved to sweat while working or exercising and spoke often of the salutary effects of perspiration. If he was sick, he knew he was getting better when he started sweating; afterwards he would say, "I broke my fever." Although he never understood my interest in triathlons, I think that they appeal to me because of the sweating and the endurance factors, both part of my dad's legacy.

Hilda

When Abe met Hilda in 1934, she was a sparkling and radiant beauty. She never lost this radiance, but little by little, from the time we were born for the next thirty-five years, she gained weight until her small 5'2" frame carried between 160 and 170 pounds. Harry Row, their roomer from 1963-66, said that Hilda always worried about her weight but "I never for the life of me ever thought she'd lose any weight . . . she was cooking all the time. It just seemed an impossible situation."

In 1973 Trudy encouraged our mother to go to Weight Watchers and went regularly with her. Hilda lost forty-seven pounds from the fall of 1973 to the fall of 1974, and her appearance was dramatically transformed. She looked stunning and was further encouraged by the attention people showered on her. Throughout their years together people who knew our parents often commented on what a beautiful couple they made. As Abe worked out of the house, he received a disproportionate share of attention, but this never bothered our mom. She accepted her role in their relationship and enjoyed caring for her children and home.

Hilda is known in the family as the "social butterfly." Her original ideas as Program Chairman for the Happy 55 Club brought light into the lives of her deaf friends, much as she "cheered up" Abe day after day.

Within their marriage Hilda was an important calming influence on Abe, and she tried hard to cheer him up, especially during their early years. When he became angry or frustrated, she would often say to us, "Yes, he is hard to manage. . . it is my duty to cheer him up." Although not in the public eye, she was an important partner in the relationship, and she knew it.

As she had learned to type in high school, she became responsible for phone calls when the TTY was introduced; without her help Abe would not have benefited much from this new device. We eventually taught him how to use it, but it took him a long time to find the right keys. Harvey called him daily for about a month, and these calls typically lasted for about thirty minutes, during which Harvey sat reading the newspaper at his end of the line waiting for Abe's slow responses.

In contrast to Abe, Hilda had a variety of hobbies and talents with which she could keep herself occupied. She loved to bake and spent several days a week turning out banana cream pies, lemon meringue pies, apple pies, rhubarb pies, honey cake, chocolate chip cookies, brownies, pineapple upside-down cake, poppyseed cake, cinnamon rolls, cheese blintzes, and homemade bread (not one of these items could possibly be left out of this book). She is also a good cook; blintzes are her specialty, but we all agree that she tends to overcook her meat. She was offended when we first told her this, but now she considers it a big joke and laughs with us.

In addition to baking and cooking she learned to sew as a young girl and has produced hundreds of pieces ranging from dresses to drapes. In the early years she made all her own clothing as well as ours, until we insisted on buying clothes when we became teenagers. Later she learned to knit, and still later, Trudy's mother taught her how to crochet and do creative stitchery. She also loves to swim and has been swimming a mile two to three times a week since starting at the YWCA twenty-five years ago. She learned how to drive when

Abe, 1982, with the women in his life. From left to right, sister Lillian, sister "Dr. Lucille," and wife Hilda.

she was forty-six.

Hilda, who is known in the family as the "social butterfly," is forever arranging birthday celebrations, picnics, or card parties, and her friends think she is a wonderful hostess. She headed the Sunshine Committee of the Happy 55 Club many times over the years and her original ideas for programs added sparkle to the lives of her deaf friends, just as she managed to cheer up Abe. When Abe and Hilda began to travel she made the arrangements. Abe, initially always reluctant about the new adventure, would thank her afterwards for "pushing" him.

For over ten years now, Hilda has taken responsibility for organizing the theatre parties for CTM's Signed Performances; she spends hours on the TDD describing the new play, encouraging friends to bring their grandchildren, and taking reservations. Without her persistence Abe never would have benefited as he did from this enrichment.

Both Eva and Trudy remember Hilda's great help after the birth of each grandchild. At first, reminiscent of the days when she cared for us, she insisted on sleeping in the baby's bedroom with her hand on the crib, because she felt more secure depending on her own perception of movement than on our hearing. She usually stayed several weeks, cooking and helping to care for the older children while the young mothers tended to the newest baby. Abe would join her for each Bris, but after the ceremony he would return to Madison alone so as not to miss his work.

Hilda never shied away from challenges, even from earliest childhood when she experimented with playing the violin. In 1985 she was called to serve as a juror in the Dane County Circuit Court. Our first reaction was to respond that she could not comply because she was deaf; however, she wanted us to explore the possibility of serving with the help of a Sign Language interpreter. It was agreed by the Court that this could be done, and we believe that she became the first deaf person in the State of Wisconsin to perform jury duty. Jury Clerk Shirley Mork said, "This is the first time we've had someone who is deaf who is willing and wants to serve."

Harvey: No description of my mother would be complete without relating how much fun she is to tease. As a child I loved to move around the living room as if I were dribbling a basketball; I would then turn quickly, jump, and touch the ceiling. My mother would stomp her foot, complaining about the "fingerprints" on the ceiling, and demand that I agree to paint the ceiling! In later years Abe and all the grandsons regularly repeated the same moves, and by then she only pretended to be upset. We knew that she loved it. A few years before my dad died, the whole family lifted her up and forced her to touch the ceiling, which she did, giggling like a young girl.

Grandchildren

Abe felt fortunate to have his grandchildren nearby, and they were similarly blessed to be near him as they grew up. Harvey's four sons saw their grandparents almost every day — Abe and Hilda attended their soccer games, concerts, and theater productions. The two families often met at a favorite restaurant, and Abe liked splitting the check with Harvey. Abe and Hilda traveled often to Milwaukee to see Eva's children, as well.

Each grandchild has learned to fingerspell and knows basic sign. Over the years each one wrote papers or poems about his or her *Zeide* for school projects, and some of this work ended up in the "gallery." At their Bar and Bat Mitzvahs each of the grandchildren signed their speeches as they spoke. This was difficult for them to do, considering the other obligations and pressures of that day, but meant a great deal to Abe and Hilda and their deaf friends. All of our children have been very close friends from early childhood. Over a period of fifteen years each one attended Camp Ramah in

Abe having fun with his grandson, Danny. He often wore a ribbed sleeveless undershirt while relaxing around the house.

Abe and Hilda keeping score while watching their grandchildren play ping pong in the chilly basement at Harvey's home. The score is 8 to 6.

Marcy (above) and Jonathan (below) chatting with their Zeide. Every grandchild has learned to fingerspell and knows basic Sign. Each one wrote papers or poems about his/ her Zeide for school projects and some of this work ended up in the "gallery."

northern Wisconsin, either as a camper or staff member. Abe and Hilda usually visited the camp during each summer and each child, in turn, showed off his *Bobe* and *Zeide* to his friends and counselors.

Every grandchild of college age went to the University of Wisconsin in Madison, so Marcy and Todd also lived in the same city with Abe and Hilda for at least four years. While in college each one set a time to have lunch with Abe in his shop, as we had done years before. Each one had a TDD and could call *Bobe* and *Zeide* to make arrangements or just to say hello. The grandchildren often joined Abe and Hilda for Sabbath meals during their college years in Madison.

Marcy majored in Early Childhood Special Education at the University of Wisconsin, and she later studied Deaf Education at Gallaudet, as both her parents did. She met her future husband, David Dropkin, while they were working at Camp Ramah after she graduated from college. They were married in Milwaukee two years later in 1983. She now works as a Parent Infant Educator at the Milwaukee Hearing Society. Remembering the model of her grandfather, she encourages young parents overcome by the deafness of their children to help them to develop their potential.

Marcy's husband, inspired by Abe and Hilda as Marcy's father had been, quickly became interested himself in deaf people and their problems with the result that Marcy and David both received master's degrees in Deaf Education from Gallaudet in 1986, as Eva and Leo had done a generation earlier. Grandson David Dropkin recently was appointed Dean of Students at the Wisconsin School for the Deaf in Delavan. How proud Abe would have been to know that David had become Dean at the school where he himself struggled to learn English, finally achieving a fifth-grade reading level! At the time of Abe's death his two-year-old great-grandson Ari already had learned to sign simple words. On the day of Abe's funeral Marcy gave birth to his second great-grandchild, a daughter, Abby.

Abe continued to show great warmth to Todd as he

grew older. He never thought of Todd as an adopted grandson, always making him feel truly loved. After Leo died, Abe provided warm support for Todd to help him deal with his loss; Todd was attending school in Madison at that time and he visited Abe often, even working with him in the shop whenever he could. Todd received his undergraduate degree in History and Hebrew from the University of Wisconsin and his master's degree from Drake University where he received the Most Outstanding Student award. He recently received a full scholarship to pursue doctoral studies in Public Administration at Florida Atlantic University. He hopes to be able to use his signing skills in his future career.

Harvey's oldest son David studied music at the University of Wisconsin in Madison. He also became very interested in deafness and took an intensive course in Sign Lan-

Abe, relaxing after a jog, with first great-grandchild, Ari Dropkin.

guage at the University of Wisconsin in Milwaukee during the summer of 1986. During his last semester at the University he chose to live with his deaf grandparents in their home, as he had grown very close to them.

Three weeks before Abe died David graduated with honors, and Abe proudly attended his graduation ceremony. Dave was Acting Cantor at Beth Israel Center, Abe's synagogue, during his last two years in college, and David's presence on the *bima* (pulpit) gave Abe immense pleasure, even though he was never able to hear David's voice. David now is studying to be a Cantor at the Jewish Theological Seminary in New York City.

Jonathan, two years younger than David, loved visiting Abe in the shop and encouraged him to develop new hobbies and interests; he sometimes jogged with Abe. They enrolled together in a mini-course in pottery at the University and Jon, along with an interpreter, helped to explain the techniques. When Abe died Jon, with one semester left at the University of Wisconsin, was applying to medical schools. After Abe's death, he moved into Hilda's home and lived with her for his last semester, helping her adjust to being alone. He graduated Phi Beta Kappa from the University and is now studying at Yale Medical School. He volunteered at a nearby school once a week where he taught his first grade inner-city class fingerspelling and some of the basic signs.

Like his brothers and cousins, Josh had a wonderful relationship with Abe as he was growing up, and Abe went to many of his plays, soccer games, and musical performances. Abe died during the night after attending Joshua's graduation with high honors from West High School. Josh recently graduated Phi Beta Kappa from the University of Wisconsin where he majored in Afro-American Studies, and he plans to enter medical school. He, too, has taken a University Sign Language course to improve his skills.

Dan loved his grandfather deeply and feels cheated that he knew him for such a short time, yet he is the only one who interacted with him from infancy. Abe attended his many

Abe in 1983 relaxing with several of his grandsons, from left to right, Todd, Jon, Josh, and David.

theatrical performances and was especially proud to see Dan at age eight as Winthrop in *The Music Man*, performed on the Oscar Mayer stage in the Civic Center before two thousand people.

Like all the grandchildren, Dan is an excellent student; he was a freshman at West High School when Abe died. He is currently a sophomore at the University of Wisconsin, and he hopes to be a professional actor someday. He wishes that Abe could have lived to see him on stage as an adult.

Golden Anniversaries

On February 24, 1985, our parents celebrated their fiftieth wedding anniversary, and nine months later, on November 1, 1985, Abe marked his fiftieth year in business on Regent Street. Both celebrations were joyous milestones that testified to a lifetime of hard work and compromise.

We began planning for the fiftieth wedding anniversary party in 1983, two years before the event. Both Hilda and Abe were in good health and we prayed that they would live long enough to see and enjoy it. In early 1984 Eva lost her husband and we knew we could not be certain that our parents would stay healthy.

We selected the Edgewater Hotel for the celebration because we thought that the central university campus location and the size of the ballroom would suit the occasion. We reserved the Allen Chase Band, a local group known for playing lively Jewish music, and arranged for Chez Vous to cater the event. Abe and Hilda's wedding picture from 1935 was reproduced on the face of the invitation, which was sent to a guest list of relatives, deaf friends, Jewish friends, our own friends, some of Abe's long-time customers, and a number of other Madison shoe repairmen, including his old competitor, John Raymond.

Over five hundred people attended the celebration. Hilda's sister Rebecca came from New York, and their former roomer and "son," Phil Lev, came from California, as did their nieces Nancy Feiner and Miriam Rabinovitz.

We placed enlargements of significant photographs on large easels, and slides of hundreds of personal family photographs were projected from carousels onto screens in one part of the ballroom. The guests of honor, along with their friends, danced to the lively music, and at one point the younger guests hoisted the radiant Hilda and Abe on chairs and danced to the traditional *Hassan Kallah Mazel Tov*. Each grandchild presented an originally prepared story or poem to his grandparents in Sign Language, and several deaf friends signed their reminiscences. All presentations were interpreted by one of us for our parents or voiced for their hearing guests. Finally Abe and Hilda signed beautiful words of thanks. They were elated to have lived to share this day.

They received congratulatory letters from friends and relatives around the country. Their former rabbi, Max Lipschitz, wrote in part:

> *If there is any couple for whom I would go out of my way to attend this celebration, it would be for Abe and Hilda. They deserve this special tribute, not only because of their beauti-*

At Abe and Hilda's Golden Wedding Anniversary celebration in 1985, the younger guests hoisting the radiant Hilda and Abe on chairs dance to the traditional Hassan Kallah Mazel Tov.

Reunion between Abe and his good friend and former roomer, Phil Lev ("Sonny Boy"). Phil travelled from California to attend the fiftieth wedding anniversary celebration.

227

As talking and signing simultaneously is difficult, Harvey speaks to his parents at their anniversary through the interpreting of "best signer," Eva. Here she signs, "When I was a little boy . . . "

Marianna and John Kuglitsch, Abe and Hilda's best friends for twenty-five years, signing memories of their friendship. Sadly, Marianna passed away from a brain tumor one year before Abe died.

ful marriage, but because of their wisdom and devotion in bringing up two beautiful children. Their life has been heroic and I salute them for the love they have exhibited for each other as well as their children and family.

They even received a letter from a cousin in Russia who had never met Abe, but who had heard about him through the stories told by his own mother and grandmother who had known Abe before he left Russia. Translated into English, it reads in part:

Dear Abe, I love and respect all of you. My mother and grandmother used to tell me about you. You are very smart and you look very noble to me. You have clever eyes. I know that all your family are very friendly to each other. On the day of your Golden Anniversary, when you all get together, I wish you all best things that exist on earth . . . .

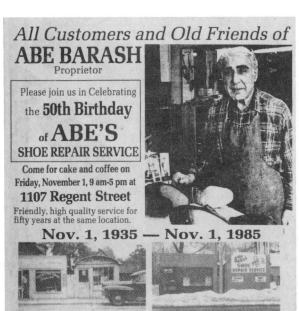

The newspaper ad announcing an open house to be held at Abe's shop in celebration of fifty years in business on November 1, 1985. On that day Abe received citations from the Governor and from the Wisconsin State Senate. Abe's Shoe Repair Service had become a Madison institution.

Nine months later an open house was held at Abe's shop on Regent Street in celebration of his fifty years of doing business at that location. Through newspaper announcements and a paid ad, old friends and customers were invited for coffee and cake. The day was bleak and sheets of rain poured down, but more than one hundred people stopped in to wish Abe their best.

On that rainy afternoon he was presented with a citation from the Governor, and State Senator Fred Risser attended, bringing with him a citation prepared by the Senate of the State of Wisconsin. These marks of official recognition and other expressions of love from the community helped Abe to comprehend that Abe's Shoe Repair Service had indeed become a Madison institution and he, a respected citizen.

CHAPTER 12

DECLINE

Our father had become deaf at a time and place in which doctors and medicines were not available. Fate had robbed him of language, and he was ultimately able to achieve only a fifth to sixth grade reading level. He made great attempts to improve his reading and vocabulary, but never had enough leisure time or financial security to succeed. He constantly asked himself what his life might have been like if he could hear.

He compensated for his loss by sheer hard work and came to measure his success in very concrete ways. After he repaired a pair of shoes, he could see and appreciate the result immediately; he had made an old, worn pair of shoes look new. His customers were pleased with his work, which gave him further reinforcement. He was hurt if a customer was not satisfied, and if he accidentally cracked the thin spiked heel of a woman's shoe, he would be terribly upset. We thought he was overly sensitive, but we see now how much he loved his work and the knowledge that he did it well.

The money he earned proved to him that his work was of value, and through his earnings he became more secure. He was able to support his family and he helped us go to college. Although he hadn't been able to go himself, helping us, and later his grandchildren, gave him special satisfaction. We knew that if anything were to prevent him from succeeding financially, significant problems might ensue.

Health

Aside from the illness in infancy that had caused him to be deaf, Abe had been blessed with good health. Hard work had made his hands strong and powerful. Whenever his friends and customers commented on his large muscles and strong hands, he would smile modestly.

In later years he observed that his muscles had become smaller and that he tired more easily. Harry Row, who had roomed in our home in the 1960s, recalls that when he came back to Madison to visit, Abe spoke to him of these changes:

> At the time that I was living there, he seemed very proud of his strength. We regularly checked each other's muscles. [Later] he talked about feeling tired and said that he didn't feel like he had the same strength and vitality.

Whenever Abe had medical problems he became exceedingly alarmed, because he knew that he had to remain healthy to do his work. He was very upset about the episode of double vision in 1976 and the heart rhythm problem in 1977; both of these problems indicated physical decline and contributed to his 1978 depression. After he began jogging, he looked and felt better.

Except for some minor arthritic problems, he remained in good health until about the time of the fiftieth anniversary celebration in his shoe shop in 1985. During the eighteen months before his death, arthritis began to affect his hands, and his shoulders became noticeably stooped. He was clearly aware that changes were occurring, as work became increasingly difficult for him. He looked and felt much older. We discussed the possibility of retirement, but he was not interested. To escape boredom, Abe would need to be busy with a hobby and he had none. He decided that it would be best for him to continue in the shop, but he planned to reduce his hours. We hoped that he would remain healthy enough to continue to work in his shop until he died, agreeing with a long-time customer who privately said to Harvey:

> His shoe shop is his castle . . . and he is the king in his kingdom there. Don't ever make him leave it; it will be fitting for him to die as lord of his castle.

The Last Weeks

For the first time any of us could remember, we observed a subtle change in his spirit during the winter months prior to his death. Our father had never been one to bother others about how he felt. On the contrary, whenever we became sick, he had ministered to our needs with one of his many home remedies. His favorites included tea and honey, a sip of brandy, long underwear, or Vick's Vaporub. Whenever he held us in his arms or rubbed us with his warm hands, he always provided the necessary tenderness to make us begin to feel better.

But now he began to complain steadily about his arthritis. He experienced pain in his shoulders, wrists, hands, and fingers. The small joints in his hands swelled up and became stiff. He did not eat well and he complained that he felt weak. He found it difficult to hold his tools and to operate his machinery, but he still went to work every day. He wanted to keep doing excellent work and satisfying his customers, and even though he worked more slowly, the quality of his finished product did not suffer.

We knew that he was not well and we talked with him often, telling him to keep his spirits up, for we fully expected him to improve as he had before. We had no reason to believe that this time would be different. He saw his doctor and was told that he had a mild anemia associated with his arthritis.

His sedimentation rate was elevated, but other tests for inflammatory arthritis were negative. He underwent additional studies, including gastroscopy and colonoscopy, searching for a reason for the change in the way he felt. All proved negative for serious disease. Abe was given one of the newer anti-inflammatory medications as treatment for his arthritis and he improved slightly.

It was no surprise to us that in the process of his medical workup he became the darling of the nurses and staff at the Jackson Clinic and Methodist Hospital, primarily because of his warm and gracious manner. Those who interacted with him immediately sensed something special about this kind man, who smiled easily and entrusted himself entirely to their care. He, in turn, was sure that everything done for him was done thoroughly and in his best interest. The trust that developed between Abe and the medical staff was beautiful to witness.

In the few weeks before his death, a number of significant life-cycle events occurred which should have been a source of great joy to him, but because he was preoccupied with his illness and his mental state, they were not. At the very time that his life was richest, he began letting go.

Three weeks before he died, David, his eldest grandson, graduated with Honors from the University of Wisconsin. Ten days later, Harvey took Abe with him when he addressed the Madison West High School Honors Convocation. In that address Harvey paid tribute to his father who had worked in silence in his shoe shop on Regent Street for over fifty years. A Sign Language interpreter conveyed Harvey's words to Abe in the language that he understood best. Later that same night the family celebrated the sixteenth birthday of Abe's youngest grandson, Danny, and a few days later Harvey and his wife celebrated their twenty-third wedding anniversary with a dinner at Abe's home.

On the last Friday night before his death Abe's large family gathered together to celebrate the Sabbath and as usual there were guests; at his table that night was Nobel

Laureate Howard Temin and his family. The next morning, the synagogue sponsored a joyous celebration in honor of David, who had served as the lay Cantor and was leaving to pursue a formal course of studies at the Cantorial Institute in New York. As David had chosen to live in Abe and Hilda's home during his final semester of college, he held a special place in their hearts. Many of Abe's deaf friends attended that Sabbath service and Eva served as interpreter.

On the next day, Sunday, on his last afternoon, Abe attended Josh's high school graduation. Harvey interpreted the speeches, and following the official ceremony the family went out for a celebration dinner. Finally, Abe was looking forward to the birth of his second great-grandchild, as his granddaughter Marcy was due to give birth in early June.

Harvey: During those three weeks before his death, my dad had begun to complain about the vision in his right eye. I thought that his current eyeglass prescription should be checked, as this had not been done for several years. My dad was concerned that he might be developing a cataract, a not unusual occurrence for people of his age. He knew that his sister-in-law, Rebecca, had recently had cataract surgery and worried that he, too, might need to have such an operation. I was about to leave with my son Jonathan on a trip East to look at medical schools so nothing was done immediately.

When I returned a week later, my dad began to complain again about poor vision in his right eye, but this time he was more insistent. He was having trouble operating his machines at work and found it necessary to close his right eye whenever precision work was required. He described what sounded to me like double vision. We made arrangements for an immediate consultation on Memorial Day, because I thought he might have a detached retina. Abe was grateful for the attention and concern of the eye doctor, who agreed to see him on an emergency basis that very day. This was again a special situation which developed in response to a special man who was deeply respected by those who had contact with him.

My dad's shoe repair shop was located one block from the Davis-Duehr Eye Clinic, and Dr. Myers, the eye doctor who specialized in detached retinas, had known about Abe for years and had stopped in the shop from time to time with shoes for him to repair. He was most willing to come to the clinic to accommodate Abe.

Arrangements were made to meet the doctor at the eye clinic instead of in the Emergency Room; in that way Dr. Myers could use specialized equipment that would help him to study the eye more carefully. When we entered the building, the alarm system went off accidentally and Dr. Myers, wearing casual clothes on this holiday morning, went to turn it off. My dad asked when the *doctor* would arrive. He had mistaken Dr. Myers for the janitor because of the way he was dressed and the fact that at first he was taking care of the alarm system and not the patient.

Unfortunately, however, this "janitor" eye surgeon had ominous news for my father. He did not have a cataract nor did he have a detached retina, both of which are conditions that usually can be corrected. Instead, the doctor found that Abe was nearly blind in one eye, with the prospect of possible permanent blindness in the other eye as well. The suspected diagnosis was temporal arteritis, an inflammatory condition of the blood vessels to the brain and to the eye which can cause irreversible blindness. This is due to a blockage of blood flow to the main nerve of the eye.

The inflammatory arthritis that had been bothering Abe for several months may well have been connected with the later development of blindness in his right eye, but there was no way to have predicted this with any certainty. A biopsy of the temporal artery done several days later showed no definite evidence of the disease in the portion of the artery that was removed for study. The pathologist who examined the biopsy through the microscope also knew Abe, and had been his customer for years. His feelings for Abe prompted him to cut numerous additional sections of the tissue, and he studied over twelve hundred sections trying to make a diagnosis.

As is true of so many diagnoses in medicine, the data did not lead directly to an unquestioned conclusion. However, the weight of the evidence in Abe's case favored the diagnosis of temporal arteritis. The findings within the eye indicated that Abe would be permanently blind in his right eye, and there was concern that the same condition would occur on the opposite side, causing the left eye to become blind as well. The doctor gave him large doses of steroids, in an attempt to prevent the condition from spreading. The medical literature suggested that the occurrence of disease in both eyes could be as high as fifty per cent.

At first our father did not fully understand the significance of this diagnosis. He was saddened by the loss of vision, but did not accept the fact that his blindness was permanent. He believed that the medicine he was taking would help, and he expected to see again in time.

The last two weeks of his life were filled with questions. He often asked why the medicine wasn't working and why he wasn't improving. We explained again that he would not get better and that the medicine he was taking was for the "good" eye — to prevent him from losing vision in that eye too. Slowly he began to realize that this was a permanent condition. Along with that knowledge and understanding, he began to lose his will to live.

For the first time in our lives we saw our father give up. He stopped fighting; he stopped struggling and striving. This was entirely out of character for him. In the past he had worked harder in response to adversities and had eventually prevailed. The reason for his resignation this time is not hard to understand. Our father had always been determined never to be dependent on others. As permanent blindness in one eye became a fact, he began to notice that he was losing the vision in his other eye. His complaints became even more bitter when he realized that he could not see well through the presumably unaffected left eye. He was retested, and although he was assured that there was no measurable evidence of further loss on that side, he insisted that he could not see at all on the right and that he was losing his vision on the left.

Harvey: My dad continued to go to work every day, but he made more and more mistakes. He began to test his vision by first covering his right eye with one hand and then his left eye with the other hand. Following this he would put on his special glasses with a cover over the right lens. Then he would raise the glasses up onto his forehead and back down onto the bridge of his nose. He repeated this sequence hundreds of times. I saw him doing this one day through the shop window as I drove by. It made me so unspeakably sad that I cried.

I usually had lunch with my dad on my afternoon off from work at the hospital, and I stopped there as usual on the Wednesday before he died. On that occasion I found my father in a very despondent mood. He was looking at some shoes that had been scuffed by his Landis stitcher and then he showed me several large cuts on his fingers He was visibly shaken. For the first time he was afraid of this large and powerful machine, with its big curved needles. For nearly fifty years he had used it to resole thousands of old, worn-out shoes. The very machine that he had loved and cared for had become an object of fear for him.

He cried for a long time that afternoon in his shoe shop. He asked again and again what he would do now that he could no longer repair shoes. He said, "What will I do? I can't see. I can't work. I'm worth nothing. I don't want to depend on you. I can't see. I can't work." He recognized that he would be fully dependent on others without his ears and without his eyes, and it was abhorrent to him. The thought of no longer being productive, of being dependent on others, and afraid of his own machinery was overwhelming. He was terrified by the the loss of control over his own life and the prospect of becoming useless.

Abe continued to go to work on Thursday and Friday of the last week of his life, but he refused to accept shoes for repair. He turned away all the shoes that were brought to him, explaining to his customers that he couldn't see well enough to repair them. He knew somehow that he would never return to his beloved shop again. His grandson David visited him in the shop on the last Friday, and Abe told him that he did not want to continue living. It was impossible for David to lift his grandfather's spirits.

On Saturday he attended the celebration for David in the synagogue. Many of his lifelong deaf friends were there, but he did not participate in the service as usual. He seemed confused and removed from the festivities. He refused an *aliyah* (call to the Torah), an honor that he otherwise cherished.

Instead he complained about his vision problem and focused inwardly. In the afternoon he discussed over and over again questions about his future with us, with his sister Lillian, and with his grandson Todd. When Eve and Todd left for Milwaukee, he trembled, crying hard as he hugged them.

On Sunday morning he awoke and tried to mow his lawn. The mower was not working properly and he was unable to fix it. When Harvey came to visit him, bringing morning buns, one of Abe's favorite foods for Sunday morning brunch, Abe was upset and frustrated. He was unwilling to discuss anything but his failing abilities. Later Jonathan stopped by and went for a walk with him, trying to lift his spirits, but he responded only briefly and again became preoccupied with his illness.

On Sunday afternoon he attended Josh's graduation, followed by dinner with the family. Throughout the ceremony he tried desperately to pay attention, but in fact he seemed to be confused, distant, and apart. The same was true at the celebration dinner. Nothing we did could cheer him up. The sparkle was gone from his eyes.

That night he went to bed in a tormented state. He was extremely depressed. He knew that he could not hear and he feared that soon he would not be able to see. He felt helpless and dependent. He understood that without his eyes and his ears he would no longer be free.

On Monday morning, the first morning of the next regular workweek, Abe Barash did not awaken. He would never go to his beloved shop again.

EULOGY FOR ABRAHAM BARASH

June 9, 1987
by Rabbi Charles Feinberg
Beth Israel Center, Madison, Wisconsin

When I think of Abe Barash, I think of the following biblical passage, which comes after the story of the golden calf. Moses comes down from the mountain. He sees the people dancing, worshiping this animal figure wrought out of gold. Moses breaks the tablets, but God wants to destroy the people and start all over. Moses, in his greatest hour, persuades God to relent, to have pity and compassion on his people. New tablets are made. The covenant between God and the people of Israel is patched up. The Bible continues:

> And he was there with the Lord forty days and forty nights; he ate no bread and drank no water; and he wrote down on the tablets the terms of the covenant, the Ten Commandments. So Moses came down from Mount Sinai. And as Moses came down from the mountain bearing the two tablets of the Covenant, Moses was not aware that the skin of his face was radiant, since he had spoken with God. Aaron and all the Israelites saw that the skin of Moses' face was radiant; and they shrank from coming near him. But Moses called to them, and Aaron and all the chieftains in the assembly returned to him, and Moses spoke to them. Afterwards all the Israelites came near, and he in-

structed them concerning all that the Lord had imparted to him on Mount Sinai. And when Moses had finished speaking with them, he put a veil over his face. Whenever Moses went in before the Lord to speak with Him, he would leave the veil off until he came out; and when he came out and told the Israelites what he had been commanded, the Israelites would see how radiant the skin of Moses' face was. (Exodus 34:28-35)

It is not far-fetched to compare Abe Barash to Moses. Like Moses, Abe was born in a country that hated Jewish people. Like Moses, Abe at an early age was overcome by a disability that caused him the greatest anguish and frustration. And like Moses, Abe fled his birthplace, came to accept his disability, thereby overcoming it, and became a leader of his family and of our community. Above all, just as Moses is described here, Abe's face shone. His radiance was due not only to his handsome appearance and bearing. He was such a handsome man. But his radiance was profoundly spiritual. Abe possessed a glorious spirit; a spirit that was generous, compassionate, full of pride, passionately independent.

It was not always so. Abe was born in Russia in 1913. As a very young child, he contracted a disease that left him profoundly deaf. His sister Lillian was also overcome by this disease but her hearing loss was not as severe or absolute as Abe's was. After the First World War, Abe along with his mother and his sister Lillian, came to the United States. When they arrived in New York, Abe as a young boy of seven or eight, faced his first test. The immigration authorities screened out all immigrants who were mentally incompetent or disabled. Abe was taken without his mother to a room where he was observed and tested. Abe passed that test even though he had no language with which to communicate. His grace, his humor, and his beautiful eyes overcame the doubts or suspicions of the authorities.

The family settled in Fond du Lac. When Abe was

fourteen, he was enrolled at the Wisconsin School for the Deaf in Delavan. Up until then, Abe had no language. His parents spoke Yiddish in the home, English was spoken to him in the street and at school. At Delavan, he learned a language. He learned to speak with his hands and listen with his eyes. His hands were beautiful to watch — large, strong, and incredibly expressive.

At Delavan, Abe learned the trade of shoe repair and shoemaking that became such an important part of his life. Most importantly, Abe learned or was born with an extraordinary capacity for work. From the time he left school in the early 1930s to the day of his death, Abe always worked. Work for him was not only the means to support himself and his family — work was an essential element of his identity.

In 1934, Abe met Hilda Nathenson. It was an arranged date. Both families heard about the other and were anxious to fix them up. But although Hilda had a severe hearing loss, she did not know Sign as Abe did. Hilda was educated to speak and to read lips. Hilda had to learn Abe's language in order to communicate with him. But this was only one of the many obstacles they had to overcome.

In 1935, Abe and Hilda were married. That was not easy. The Congregation would not permit them to be married in the synagogue. Although Abe and Hilda came from traditional Jewish homes, they were not allowed to have a wedding like other couples. Instead, they were married in the Workman's Circle Building in Madison, not far from here.

They were married in the most difficult of times. It was the middle of the Depression. Abe opened his shop fifty-two years ago and he never closed it. Even though there was little work, Abe managed to keep it going. He would go door to door, looking for shoes to repair. He would work ten to twelve hours in a cramped building without much heat, and no bathroom. He would stand at his machines and do his work. While he was standing at those machines, he would ask himself, "Why was I cursed with this disability? I could have been something else. I could have been a doctor, I could have been a lawyer, I could have been more successful." During those years Abe worked day and night and was filled with anger and frustration.

Eva and Harvey remember that anger, they remember that frustration. They remember how poor they were and they remember how hard their father worked and how devoted he was to them and to the rest of his family, especially to Hilda's parents and to his own parents. They remember how much pride both Hilda and Abe took in their accomplishments. Eva played the violin as a child and they went to every concert, every recital, even though they could not hear. They went to every school and synagogue performance their children were in, even though they had to sit in silence and not understand what was being said.

But at some point, Abe stopped fighting himself and his deafness. At some point, and it is hard to pinpoint when it was, Abe began to accept that he was deaf. And at some point, he became less frustrated and less angry at God and the imperfections and agony of His creation. When that happened, Abe became our Moses, a leader, a spiritual presence in our community.

Abe inspired Eva to pursue a career in deaf education. Abe inspired Eve's late husband, Leo, z'l (may his memory be a blessing), to pursue a career in deaf education. Eva told me that whenever she is interpreting, she sees her father before her. She wants to make sure that those who are watching her sign understand everything that a hearing person is understanding. Abe inspired his granddaughter Marcy and her husband David Dropkin to pursue careers in deaf education. Abe inspired David to devote a whole summer to learning Sign. Abe inspired a whole host of people to become acquainted with the rudiments of Sign Language.

Most importantly, Abe taught others about what it means to be deaf, to be cut off from the hearing world, and how terribly lonely and frightening that can be. By teaching us this, he helped us to reach out to the hearing impaired. No longer will deaf families be excluded from synagogues and other community institutions. No longer will deaf couples have to find a place to be married. No longer will the deaf be ignored when synagogue honors are being handed out. In this way, Abe was our Moses, he led us out of an Egypt, the Egypt of ignorance of and insensitivity to the needs of the hearing-impaired and of other disabled people.

Abe has been blessed with a wonderful family. Abe and Hilda have been married for fifty-two years. For fifty-two years each stood by the other, even under the most difficult of circumstances. Abe and Hilda loved each other deeply and profoundly. It was always so pleasing to me to look at them together, to see the love that radiated from them. That love encompassed their children and their children's children, and their great-grandchildren. It has always been so pleasing to me to see how Abe's grandchildren gave him such respect and love. They loved to stop in his shop, have lunch with him, and learn from him. Today Marcy is supposed to give birth to her second child. This is an extraordinary moment — feeling the sorrow of death and the joy of birth.

That love was felt every Friday night when the family gathered to celebrate the Sabbath together. Abe would sign the Kiddush with his hands and fingers, and then bless the family. He would bless all his family, and then remind them to be aware of those who were less fortunate. Like Moses, he would remind them of the poor, of the homeless, of the disabled, the deaf, the blind, of those who were dying from starvation. He would bless the guests in attendance. And guests came so very often. Abe Barash could never forget what it means to suffer. His great achievement is that he taught his family and so many friends what it means to suffer and how important it is to reach out to those in need.

I close with one more story. Eva remembers entering the shop and finding her father reading the Bible. He was contemplating the phrase, "God is my rock." Looking up at her, he said, "I am a rock, I feel like a rock." Abe truly was a rock, our Rock of Gibraltar. His strength, his sense of purpose, his fierce independence, were chiseled into every feature of his body. Indeed, he was a rock. But the verse was not fully quoted. And I'd like to finish the verse: "My rock, in whom there is no unrighteousness."

His memory shall surely be a blessing and source of inspiration to you, Harvey and Trudy, Eva, Todd, Marcy and David, David, Jon, Josh, Danny, and to your children's children, and to their children.

But his memory will also be a blessing and source of inspiration to all of us who knew him and loved him so very much.

Amen.

EPILOGUE

Nearly all Jewish funerals are conducted in a funeral home or at the graveside. Our father was given the honor of a funeral in the synagogue. This honor is usually reserved for extremely devout and pious Jews or for individuals who have made substantial monetary contributions to Jewish causes, neither of which Abe had been capable of doing. Recognized leaders of the Jewish community are also given this honor, and although Abe wasn't a community leader in the usual sense, he was certainly a leader in another important way, as the eulogy given by Rabbi Charles Feinberg made so clear.

Because of his deafness Abe had never heard music during his lifetime. He did feel its vibrations, and often danced to the rhythm of these vibrations. Once during a solo violin concert by a friend in his home, he stood next to the violinist while she was playing and placed his hand on the instrument so he could "feel" the music through his fingers. He had always wished that he could hear the voice of his eldest grandson, David, who had chosen to become a Cantor, the messenger *(shaleach)* between the Jewish people and their God. He frequently attended concerts and services when David sang, but obviously had never heard his voice.

The synagogue was flooded with bright sunlight as David sang *El Malei Rachamin* ("Exalted, Compassionate

God"), the traditional prayer in memory of the dead, while his grandfather's body lay in the casket nearby. Someone present that afternoon mused that for the first time Abe, in spirit, just possibly might have experienced the joy of listening to the full, rich, resonant voice of his eldest grandson, the congregation's Messenger to God.

One hour after Abe's burial his second great-grandchild was born. She was given the name Avigial after her grandfather. In Hebrew this name means "joy of my father." Her English name is Abby, a direct phonetic linkage to Abe's name. In the Jewish tradition some believe that the soul (*nefesh*) lives on after the physical death of a person. Although we do not suggest seriously that his soul is embodied within Abby, we do know that he lives on in each of us that knew him. He was a strong and important influence on his family's character, and he made a significant imprint upon the many others who knew him during his lifetime.

His ideas, values, work ethic, and spirit will continue to influence his children, his children's children, and their children from generation to generation.

AFTERWORD

Not long after our father's death, we decided, together with our mother, to sell his beloved shop. We hoped to find someone who would carry on the shoe repair business and continue his legacy, but we didn't dare dream that we would ever find anyone like our dad to run the shop. It would have been enough for us to have it continue as a shoe repair shop.

We contacted his former competitor, Salvadore Franco, as he had once expressed interest in purchasing the shop if our dad ever retired. He was noncommital and said that he would be interested in it only as storage space and he didn't seem to want to make an offer. We contacted several other Madison shoe repairmen for leads without much success. We placed ads in the Madison newspapers and in the national trade magazine, *Shoe Service*. Several people inquired, but no one showed real interest.

After several weeks we looked into the possibility of selling the property outright to be used for some other purpose, based on its land value and its location on Regent Street. At about that time in early August, two months after our dad died, Gregory Kleiman made an inquiry on behalf of his brother-in-law, Mikhail (Mike) Soroka. Although we did not know them well, we had become acquainted with the Kleimans when they settled in Madison after emigrating here from Russia ten years earlier. We were vaguely aware that Gregory's wife had a brother who had come to this country recently and that he operated a shoe repair shop on the east side of town. In fact, we had seen several ads that he had placed in the synagogue newsletter, the *Beth Israel Centerite*. Once, after seeing the ad, our dad had remarked that he was happy his business was so good that he didn't have to advertise.

We learned from Gregory that Mikhail had been struggling to eke out a living on the east side for the past five years, operating his shop from two different locations. Both times he had just begun to establish himself when he had lost his lease and been forced to move. The property owners either wanted more money or they wanted to rent to a business that was cleaner than shoe repairing. He was about to lose his lease again and he was interested in our dad's shop.

Mikhail was nearly fifty years old and bore little physical resemblance to Abe, but when we met him we noticed a definite likeness: he had bright, penetrating eyes, smiled warmly, and had language problems. He tried to make himself understood as we showed him around the shop, but his wife had to interpret for him because of his poor English. As we grew to understand him better, we learned that he could not read or write English although he spoke Russian well. We were attracted to this Russian Jewish immigrant and secretly hoped that he might end up in our dad's shop, even though the whole business of selling the shop was heart-wrenching.

The negotiations with Mikhail went smoothly, and we helped him to apply for a loan by preparing a detailed inventory of the shop and taking photographs of the machinery. The Madison Development Corporation was offering guaranteed loans to people like Mikhail, who were trying to establish small businesses. When the Corporation finally approved the loan application, it was a happy day. We felt our dad's warm presence at the closing in our lawyer's office, and we were especially touched when our attorney, Tom Hoffner, presented Mike with some shoes in need of repair for his first piece of work in the new shop. As Attorney Hoffner was our dad's former customer, these shoes symbolized the transfer of his confidence from Abe to Mike.

We were attracted to this Russian Jewish immigrant and secretly hoped that he might end up in our dad's shop. Mike offered to leave our favorite picture of Abe on the wall of his shop; it still hangs there four years later. He also promised our mother, hugging her, to fix her shoes for free for as long as she lived.

In turn, Mike offered to place our favorite picture of Abe at work on the wall of his shop. It still hangs there four years later in memory of our father, along with the citations presented to Abe by the Governor and by the State Senate of Wisconsin. Mike also promised our mother, hugging her, that he would fix her shoes "for free" for as long as she lived. In return, she has made it part of her regular routine to bring him samples of her freshly baked pies and cakes.

> **Harvey:** I witnessed the following incident one day while standing at the counter in Mike's (formerly Abe's) shop. A customer who had heard about, but had never met, my dad entered the shop and began writing on a pad of paper describing what he wanted done with his shoes. Mike, realizing that the customer thought he was dealing with Abe, stopped him, declaring, "I can't read English. Please speak." Imagine how strange I felt, recalling that my dad always wrote, "I can't hear. Please write."

We were astonished to learn recently that Mike's mother had grown up in the small village of Delinkas. Although she had not known Abe's family personally, her older sister knew all about the deaf shoe repairman in Madison, Wisconsin. When this sister learned that Mike had purchased Abe's shop, she wrote to Mike's mother from New York, declaring that she had known Abe when he was a small boy in Delinkas. Not only had she known him, but she had traveled from Antwerp to Ellis Island on the same ship with the Barash family, and was able to describe the little deaf boy's clever antics on board the ship!

It seems mysterious and wonderful that Abe, whose early roots were in the small *shtetl* of Delinkas and who had established new, deep roots in the Madison community, made way fifty-two years later for another Russian Jewish immigrant who could trace his roots from Delinkas to Madison.